MW00514202

# NEW YORK'S 50 BEST

# PLACES
# TO EAT
# SOUTHERN

## WHERE TO FIND HOPPIN' JOHN, GRITS, BARBECUE, AND FRIED EVERYTHING

**BRUCE LANE & SCOTT WYATT**

CITY & COMPANY • NEW YORK

Library of Congress Cataloging-in-Publication Data
Lane, Bruce.
New York's 50 best places to eat Southern: where to find hoppin'
john, grits, barbecue, and fried everything/by Bruce Lane & Scott
Wyatt.
p.cm.
Includes Index.
ISBN 1-885492-57-X
1. Restaurants–New York (State)–New York– Guidebooks. 2.
Cookery, American–Southern style.
3. New York (N.Y.)–Guidebooks.
I. Wyatt, Scott. II Title.
TX907.3.N72N45
1998
847.95747'1–dc21
98-2928
CIP

Publisher's Note:
Neither City & Company nor the authors have any interest, finan-
cial or personal, in the locations listed in this book. No fees were
paid or services rendered in exchange for inclusion in these pages.

**DEDICATED TO THE
REVIVAL AND PRESERVATION
OF SOUTHERN FOOD**

# ADVANCE PRAISE FOR
## NEW YORK'S 50 BEST PLACES
## TO EAT SOUTHERN

"Uprooted and dispatched to the land of egg creams and bagels, every transplanted Southerner in New York City has one thing in common—we are always hungry. We'll take some strange detours lusting for barbecue and end up in some mighty odd places searching for grits and country gravy, often with frustrating results. That search is now over. This is a reference book whose time has come. In the immortal words of Scarlett O'Hara, I'll never go hungry again."

—Rex Reed

"A train ride took me out of South Carolina as a little girl, but I can still remember feasting on fried catfish sandwiches as the South slipped behind me. To this day, fried chicken, grits, collard greens—with no fatback, of course—and sweet potato pie are the foods of home that I cherish and crave. *New York's 50 Best Places to Eat Southern* can lead everyone to those comforts. That's such a wonderful thing, because Southern food is food that warms the heart."

—Eartha Kitt

"I sure wish I'd had this book when I lived in New York. Even reading it now that I'm back down home makes my mouth water. It would be silly to go to New York from North Carolina to eat Southern food, but this book makes me want to do it."

—John Shelton Reed, author of *1001 Things Everyone Should Know About the South* and *Whistling Dixie*

"This is your Duncan Hines ticket to down-home cooking in the Big Apple, your Gotham Underground Gourmet, your classic entrée to entrees you'd never have dreamed of finding anywhere north of Richmond. *New York's 50 Best Places to Eat Southern* is more unerring than a hush-puppy-sniffing hound. It'll flat get you to the table quicker than you can flip a hoecake. With this bundle of choices, I'll never miss a meal in Manhattan again—or Queens, or Brooklyn."

—John Egerton, author of *Southern Food* and *Side Orders*

"This book is right about the places in it where I have eaten, and I intend to eat in as many of the others as I can before I die."

—Roy Blount, Jr.

# CONTENTS

"SURE, SURE I HEARD OF GRITS. I JUST
ACTUALLY NEVER SEEN A GRIT BEFORE."

—JOE PESCI, *MY COUSIN VINNY*
DALE LAUNER, SCREENWRITER

# PREFACE

▰▰▰▰▰▰▰▰▰▰▰▰▰▰▰▰▰▰▰▰▰▰▰

We came, we saw, we ate, we wrote.

I t's that simple. We're just two sons of the South who know good down-home cooking when it's put on the table in front of us. What's on these pages is what we found to be the best of the best, the hottest okra and oxtails from New York's top 50 Dixie domains.

Alas, our ever-tightening clothing prevented us from trying everything on every menu (though we were sorely tempted to just buy new wardrobes). So if we don't recommend a dish, you're on your own. Remember, too, that everything changes: chefs come and go, hours vary, restaurants move. It's always a good idea to call ahead.

Of course, if you discover a gem that may have eluded us, we'd love to hear from you. For us, the search for spectacular Southern food is never-ending.

# INTRODUCTION

▰▰▰▰▰▰▰▰▰▰▰▰▰▰▰▰▰▰▰▰▰▰▰

**A**re there even 50 Southern restaurants in New York? Although it might seem collards and corn pone would be as scarce as hen's teeth in the land of pizza parlors and Chinese takeout, that's simply not true. Gotham is teeming with down-home eats, some better than anything you'd likely find in the Land of Cotton. So to answer the question, we know of at least one hundred and fifty down-home kitchens in the city. The hard part wasn't finding the restaurants, it was narrowing the field.

We come by our love for Southern cuisine honestly, having been born and raised below the Mason-Dixon line. When Manhattan beckoned, we hightailed it here only to find ourselves craving the comfort of the grits and gravy we once took for granted. Dixie culture is so distinctly tied in with the rituals of eating, no refugee can escape its pull for long. From the moment we're fed that first bite of sweet potato pie while screeching in our high chairs, Southerners see food as far more than nourishment. That's why we started seeking Southern sustenance in the concrete jungle—gut instinct.

Most Southerners can and will argue until they're blue in the face about the whats, whens, wheres, and hows of our cherished regional cuisine, and, frankly, so could we. But instead of riding the fence and, bearing in mind that it's impossible to please everyone, we came up with our own set of simple criteria for the purposes of this book. The South, to our minds, stretches from West Virginia to the Florida state line and from east Texas to the Atlantic Ocean. As for sugar, we prefer our cornbread without and our iced tea either way (but never instant). And barbecue, subject of

the Great Debate, can be anything from pork to beef to lamb, as long as it at least tastes smoky and we get to choose our own poison—mustard, tomato, or vinegar sauces. They all have their merits.

We may be as blunt as an old hoe about a restaurant's ambiance and decor because they affect the whole package, but finding the best is really about the food. If a shabby shotgun shack serves up a mean mint julep with a "Howdy-do," we're hooked.

The distinct aromas and undeniably rich flavors of down-home cooking easily send the homesick mind reeling back toward country scenes, doting grandmothers, and idyllic lifestyles—not to mention pickup trucks, Wal-Mart, and big hair. That's what we love about Southern food. No matter where we roam—even the big city—it can always take us back, if just for a few brief moments. We hope you find the same.

—Bruce Lane & Scott Wyatt
New York

# ACADIA PARISH

▄▄▄▄▄▄▄▄▄▄▄▄▄▄▄▄▄▄▄▄▄▄▄▄▄▄▄

**148 ATLANTIC AVENUE**
**BET. CLINTON & HENRY STREETS**
**COBBLE HILL, BROOKLYN**
**718-624-5154**
**MAJOR CREDIT CARDS**

**MAIN COURSES: $13–$16**

**H**ard to believe that minutes outside Gotham and a short stroll from the Borough Hall subway station is a pastoral community, worlds away from the Sturm und Drang. Yet there is such a place. Along Atlantic Avenue, picturesque mom-and-pop establishments line a Main Street, U.S.A. setting. Know thy neighbor is the Golden Rule. Not surprising then that Gerald Faulk of Acadia Parish, Louisiana, would choose this locale to work his Cajun magic.

Acadia Parish is unencumbered by the trappings of Big City restaurants. On any given night, regulars greet each other by name as they maneuver through the narrow room, its tables crammed in at odd angles to accommodate as many diners as possible. The surroundings are minimal, a folksy conglomeration of tin ceilings, Mardi Gras masks, and posters of rural Acadia's own Rayne Frog and Church Point Buggy Festivals.

Appetizers are pure Louisiana, from fried oysters to popcorn crawfish. A wide-mouthed bowl piled high with jet black, steaming mussels is a popular seafood starter, as is a coffee cup full of shrimp and andouille gumbo in earthy fish stock broth with a smidgen of pungent filé spice. Bite-size morsels of blackened alligator—which tastes like perfectly charred chicken—is the one gusty delicacy to experience.

Acadia Parish blackens so expertly, they choose to ply their trade on four kinds of fish, stout cuts of Angus steak, and chops of both lamb and pork. The salmon, in particular, is sublime, smeared with a precise blend of customary spices. For something other than blackened, try the pecan-crusted chicken with its unlikely strawberry sauce or the bulky Louisiana crab cakes, browncrusted and dressed with spoonfuls of remoulade.

Then there's the catfish fillet under a blanket of cream and crawfish sauce the color of hollandaise, barely seasoned but naturally sumptuous. Wet greens and chicken liver-loaded dirty rice come on the side.

Desserts are deceptively simple but inspired, from the lemon mousse cheesecake to the decadent pumpkin pecan pie. Acadia Parish is BYOB, but the staff will happily direct you to a nearby liquor store. And that's how this area seems to work—all in the neighborhood and all in the family.

# ACME BAR & GRILL

9 GREAT JONES STREET
BET. BROADWAY & LAFAYETTE STREET
212-420-1934
VISA/MASTERCARD

MAIN COURSES: $11–$15

"An okay place to eat." That's Acme's own self-deprecating label. On one hand, that sort of off-the-wall tag could be the equivalent of wearing an antler hat in a forest full of heavily-armed food critics. On the other hand, it could be the sign of a restaurant so sure of itself it dares to shake its fluffy white tail out in the open. Place your bets on the latter.

From its corrugated tin ceiling to the gigantic Sunoco sign light fixture, Acme presents a well-planned image. The interior is a Hollywood-like replica of a backwater machine shop-turned-honky tonk: an Acme Oil Filters billboard, 999 bottles of fermenting hot sauce on the wall, empty crab meat containers brimming with

Domino's sugar packets, Louisiana's Avery Island Tabasco emblems all over the place. No stone on the dirt road has been left unturned.

Acme's acoustics rival the raucous reverberation of a cinder block warehouse. Dishes clanking yards away seem to be at the next table. Voices don't carry, they bounce. Only wild zydeco music punctuates the pandemonium. All part of the picture, darlin'.

The menu is jam-packed with more down home staples than most restaurants in the honest-to-goodness South. The list of starters reads like a Carolina cookbook—corn fritters, hush puppies, fried okra. Almost anything that moves can be had deep-fried, blackened, barbecued, or "spicy" with heaping helpings of arguably the best mashed potatoes in town, coarsely crushed but with an utterly smooth cream gravy.

Acme's barbecue sauce is so rich with dark molasses and umber spices that the soppin' wet baby back ribs are almost black; they are a must. Missing Mama? Try country smoked ham with red-eye gravy or crunchy deep-fried chicken that arrives hotter 'n' hell and as juicy as can be with gooey pecan pie for dessert. The only danger here is the old your eyes are bigger than your stomach syndrome.

Exiting Acme, it seems as if a crunching gravel parking lot full of pickup trucks and Bubbas should be beyond the door. But at the register, you suddenly notice the waiter's garage band T-shirt and patchouli oil. This is still NYU territory.

"YOU CAN TELL HOW LONG A COUPLE HAS BEEN MARRIED BY WHETHER THEY ARE ON THEIR FIRST, SECOND, OR THIRD BOTTLE OF TABASCO."
—BRUCE R. BYE

# BABY JAKE'S

▪▪▪▪▪▪▪▪▪▪▪▪▪▪▪▪▪▪▪▪▪▪▪▪▪▪▪▪▪▪▪▪▪▪▪▪▪▪

### 14 FIRST AVENUE AT 1ST STREET
### 212-254-2229
### MAJOR CREDIT CARDS

### MAIN COURSES: $10–$14

**B**aby Jake's at first appears to be a poseur trying way too hard for that certain East Village air. So garage sale chic, so kitschy, so hipper-than-thou, ripping it to shreds would be like shooting fish in a barrel. But, damn it all, the place is really good.

It's also really red—red floors, red kitchen chairs, red Formica—red napkin dispensers, for heaven's sake. Whorehouses are more demure. Beyond the maraschino mayhem are strings of plastic patio lanterns and duct-taped booths, rips caused by too many pierced bodies, no doubt. And the "artwork" ranges from doe-eyed Daisy in a misfit frame to Aunt Fanny's cubist attempts, circa 1962. As a Southern granny would say, it's uglier than a mud fence. But try as you might to laugh it off as too self-consciously shabby, the room is a real riot.

What's most amazing about Jake's is its ability to churn out kick-ass food with only two people in the smallest kitchen this side of a studio apartment. Like pulling rabbits out of a hat, the self-anointed SOUL KITCHEN (spelled out in black and white tiles) does it all before your disbelieving eyes. The miracles begin with New Orleans crab cakes with chipotle tartar sauce, salmon-filled hush puppies and cornmeal-covered oysters with a fresh-cut corn, onion, and tomato salsa.

Though salads aren't Southern (they aren't fried, are they?), Jake's offers an exception: the Bayou salad, with fried catfish, oysters, and okra in a green onion-buttermilk dressing. A mixture of remoulade and chile-horse-radish cocktail sauce makes the po' boys spectacular, if not overflowing with fried seafood fillings.

**DEEP FAT FRYING**

While most of the menu is Cajun and Creole, big-ticket dinner items are a nod to the Southwest. Some traditional choices, though, are the blackened sirloin steak with silky garlic mashed potatoes and blackened catfish cloaked in Kentucky bourbon and pecan butter sauce. Banana bread pudding with bourbon praline sauce served piping hot from the oven with whipped cream, chocolate drizzles, and a golden top lightly dusted with powdered sugar is the eye-popping finale of choice.

Baby Jake's is no poseur, it's the genuine Louisiana article at ground zero of Pretension Central. Proof positive that appearances can be deceiving.

OUTDOOR FRYING WAS OFTEN NECESSARY IN THE OLD SOUTH, AND THE SCENT ATTRACTED EVERY HOWLING HOUND IN THE COUNTY. SCOOPS OF CORN-MEAL BATTER WERE THROWN IN THE HOT FAT, THEN TOSSED TO THE DOGS WITH CRIES OF, "HUSH, PUPPIES." HUMANS, AT SOME POINT, FIGURED OUT WHAT THEY WERE MISSING.

# BAR-BE-QUE KING

**2480 EIGHTH AVENUE AT 133RD STREET**
**212-491-5000**
**CASH ONLY**

**MAIN COURSES: $5–$10**

For Southerners, barbecue can inspire religiouslike fervor. The pit is a holy place where the defense of beliefs often takes on epic, fiery proportions. Sermons are given on smoking, sauces, meats, even the appropriate accompanying bread (bow your head reverently at the mere mention of Wonder). But the owners, the Lucas family, know church is for worship and their storefront cafe, Bar-Be-Que King, is "where friends meet for good food."

Blatantly breaking the first commandment of the coals, Bar-Be-Que King's meats are not smoked. Then again, neither is most of the barbecue in Manhattan. Does it matter? Not judging by the congregating masses ordering takeout from a backlit menu board. From inside a Plexiglas booth, the cashier shouts out orders while Mr. Lucas fields oddball requests from the sidelines. The daytime "stories" play out on a black-and-white TV. In the background, comments like, "God don't like you being lazy, Pee Wee" fly from the kitchen.

It's a casual place but, in accordance with God's wishes, not lazy. Though the ribs, chicken, and pulled pork are not pit-cooked, they are quality cuts bathed in a heavenly sauce—sloppy slabs of pork ribs and rotisserie chicken arrive anointed with the dark orange,

sweet, and salty con-
coction. Deep-fried
chicken, Cornish hens,
seafood, and even pig's
feet make divine platters,
and almost all the entrees
are available as sandwiches...on white bread. Hallelujah!

Bar-Be-Que King whips up
glorious side dishes and desserts. The hot, semimashed
candied yams have a distinct apple twang. Macaroni
and cheese is riddled with pockets of dense custard and
intense, ultrasharp Cheddar. The vegetables—lima
beans, string beans, collards—taste as if they have been
simmered all morning then cloaked in smoke and seasonings. Of course, white rice with peas or gravy is a
fixture on the menu. And the homemade sweet potato
pie, with its coarsely whipped and spice-drenched filling, is downright angelic, but with an earthly crust.

So while the holier-than-thou parsons of the pit
spend their time battling the sins of the grill, the
Lucases continue to dish up superlative down-home
fare that can be had for a song. Let the choir sing!

"SOME LEGISLATORS WERE BOTHERED BY THE PENAL-
TIES [FOR NONCOMPLIANCE]. BUT IF YOU'RE EATING
BARBECUE, YOU DESERVE TO KNOW EXACTLY WHAT
YOU'RE GETTING."

—JOHN "BUBBER" SNOW,
SOUTH CAROLINA STATE REPRESENTATIVE,
ON HIS "TRUTH IN BARBECUE" LAW

# BIRDLAND

▪▪▪▪▪▪▪▪▪▪▪▪▪▪▪▪▪▪▪▪▪▪▪▪▪▪▪▪▪▪▪▪▪▪▪▪▪

### 315 W. 44TH STREET
### BET. EIGHTH & NINTH AVENUES
### 212-581-3080
### MAJOR CREDIT CARDS

### MAIN COURSES: $12–$16

There was a time when well-dressed Manhattan couples dined out at lavish Harlem clubs in the smoky glow of lamplight while jazz greats and crooners entertained. Those heady days are gone, but Birdland keeps the spirit of the supper club alive.

Birdland exists, first and foremost, for jazz, but the topnotch shows and kitchen work in perfect harmony. A multilevel, crescent-shaped dining room operates as an extension of the stage, with spotlights hung across the red ceiling and gray acoustical carpeting covering the walls. Black-and-white photos of legendary musicians line the room.

Playing on New Orleans' roots as "the jazz corner of the world," Birdland focuses more on Louisiana cooking since its move from West 105th Street. Several soul standards endure, including chicken livers, ribs, and a macaroni-and-cheese entree, but seafood takes center stage. As a warm-up, try the crawfish and crab patties, fried oysters or the misnamed catfish fritters, which are actually a duet of catfish fingers and a sweet, melodious cabbage-and-carrot slaw with Creole-spiced tartar sauce. The black-eyed pea and sweet potato soup—a sometime special—sounds like an innovative rhapsody of two Southern hits, but it's as basic as Chopsticks. For the best prelude, dig into the gleaming, buttery biscuits, the first—and finest—thing to arrive.

Birdland's house specialty is its marvelous, richly red seafood gumbo, a deep bowl of mildly spiced shrimp, silver dollar-sized scallops and a medley of fish, including pink slabs of salmon. Atlantic salmon also comes grilled and topped with a sweet potato pecan sauce, and Southern fried catfish doubles as a po' boy or a main dish with collards and black-eyed peas.

Beyond the sea are seared pork medallions in a brandy apple gravy with candied yams or an enormous portion of deep-fried chicken with smoky, simmered greens and potatoes whipped so smooth, you'll want to forego the gravy. Key lime pie is a worthy finish, but chocolate lovers should sample the Mississippi mud pie, a wedge of fudgy filling with Oreos as both topping and crust.

Birdland has a cover charge and a food minimum during performances. But unlike most jazz clubs, ordering dinner at Birdland is an experience instead of a way to reach the minimum charge. That's a rare bird.

BIRDLAND IS NAMED FOR LEGENDARY JAZZ SAXOPHONIST CHARLIE PARKER, KNOWN TO MOST SIMPLY AS "BIRD."

# BROTHER JIMMY'S

**1461 FIRST AVENUE AT 76TH STREET**
**212-288-0999**
**MAJOR CREDIT CARDS**

**MAIN COURSES: $8–$16**

If a good bottle of barbecue sauce is your idea of fine wine, then the Upper East Side is a dry county. But like a hillbilly with a homemade still, Brother Jimmy's (along with its nearby baby brother Bait Shack) provides the cure to what ails you in this pasta-packed neighborhood. They've even been known to give Southerners a White Trash Wednesday discount.

Swing open the screen door, and you'll find the founders have painstakingly re-created the hangouts of their Duke days—license plates and Tar Heel paraphernalia are the overriding decorative elements, along with rough-hewn wood and bright neon beer signs, with Lynyrd Skynyrd blaring. Add a collegiate crowd and freshly scrubbed staff, and it seems like the afternoon of The Big Game.

The toga party din fades with the arrival of the better-than-a-bread-basket coleslaw, a sweet concoction with just a touch of mayonnaise and vinegar that puts the paper-cupped Greek diner version into perspective. If you enjoy food shaped like a deep-fryer basket (and who

doesn't?), try the mound of crispy onion straws to start.

Brother Jimmy's serves up thick and hearty ribs ("no baby backs," says the menu), slow-cooked for at least eight hours and worth the wait. Both the pulled and chopped pork are hickory-smoked heaven, with sides of black-eyed peas and skins-in mashed potatoes with cream gravy to complete the platter perfectly. Try the barbecue sandwich with one of the varieties of regional sauces on the table, topped with a scoop of that crunchy coleslaw for a truly Southern delicacy.

But here's the rub—the dry rub, that is. For those who prefer this less-messy and also highly spiced version of ribs, Brother Jimmy's produces something with lots of crunch and not quite enough natural juiciness. As for other cuisines the menu explores, like Tex-Mex, salads and "healthy" stuff...well, let's just say it ain't called Brother Jimmy's BBQ and Booze for nothin'. This is a place to "put some South in yo' mouth."

SOME OTHER ALUMNI WHO KNOW A THING OR TWO ABOUT BARBECUE ARE THE FOLKS WHO SERVE IT UP ANNUALLY (ALONG WITH COLESLAW, CATFISH, AND HUSH PUPPIES) AT THE MISSISSIPPI PICNIC OF NEW YORK. OLE MISS GRADS AND TRISTATE TRANSPLANTS HAVE PUT TOGETHER AN ANNUAL SUMMER PICNIC PARTY SINCE 1979. BESIDES THE GOOD EATIN', THERE ARE SLEWS OF OH-SO-SOUTHERN CONTESTS LIKE BEST HAT, BEST PICNIC DISPLAY, AND WATERMELON SEED SPITTIN'.

# BROTHERS
# BAR-B-QUE

225 VARICK STREET AT CLARKSON STREET
212-727-2775
MAJOR CREDIT CARDS

MAIN COURSES: $9–$17

**B**rothers Bar-B-Que is a truck stop-style charmer that started its long life as a haven for barbecue afficionados and a welcome diversion for pasta-and-pizza'd-to-death city folk. Every nook and cranny of the original boomerang-shaped space was stuffed with Naugahyde booths, roadhouse remembrances and, on a nightly basis, starving, smacking admirers. Brothers was incredibly popular.

So the pillar of porkdom moved to a cavernous space nearby to accommodate the crowds. The gas station signs, mounted trophy fish, and flea-market finds came with them, though they lost a bit of the campy coziness of the original.

And Brothers Bar-B-Que is as good—if not better than—it always has been. Step inside and you know it's true; the wafting fragrance, for any Southerner, is hickory-smoked aromatherapy. Brothers slow-cooks their barbecue over hardwoods for ten to twelve hours, and they put out a bevy of meats and regional styles. Sweet and tomatoey Texas brisket and vinegar-laced North Carolina pulled pork compete for "Best of Show," as do three rib styles: Southern style, spicy

bourbon, and baby back.
Gotta love a place that
somehow juggles this many
variations without ever
dropping the ball.

Chicken is another house specialty, whether it's
the fall-off-the-bone barbecued or good ol' chicken-
fried, draped in cream gravy with mashed potatoes and
black-eyed peas—a monochromatic medley with big,
Technicolor taste. The hush puppies that kick off meals
are a deep-fried sensation with hotter 'n' jalapeño dipping sauce, and they go perfectly with a bowl of boiled
peel 'n' eat 'em shrimp. Bottomless apple pie with hifa-
lutin' raspberry sauce provides a country-come-to-
town ending.

With a fresh start in its new locale, Brothers has
an eye toward the trends of the future. The tried-and-
true are now served up right along with fancier daily
specials, and that smoker is turning out everything
from duck to salmon. For pork lovers, however, it's
Brothers' dead-on approximation of the pit and incredible sauces that keep it holding firm as a steadfast
Manhattan barbecue palace.

BARBECUE FANS IN PORK-PREFERRING REGIONS OF
THE SOUTH LOVE A GOOD PIG PICKIN'. A WHOLE
HOG IS PIT-COOKED OVER HICKORY FOR AT LEAST TEN
HOURS, BASTED IN A FAVORITE SAUCE, THEN LAID OUT
FOR PULLING, POKING, AND PRODDING BY A PARADE OF
CARNIVORES.

# B. Smith's Restaurant

■■■■■■■■■■■■■■■■■■■■■■■■■■■■■■■

771 Eighth Avenue at 47th Street
212-247-2222
Major Credit Cards

Main Courses: $13–$20

Lights! Models! Celebrities! Life's a runway, baby, and B. knows it. The former *Ebony, Mademoiselle,* and *Essence* cover girl has created a successful second career as restaurateur, cookbook author, and host of her own television show. At this supermodel's cafe, though, you won't find tofu burgers and glassy-eyed waifs who are more likely to have a rib removed than to chow down on one. B.'s original brainchild, B. Smith's, combines the taste of the Old South with European haute cuisine...in big portions. Girlfriend, there's some meat on these bones!

The soaring space that houses B. Smith's Restaurant and rooftop cafe is a reflection of the fashion world. Giant metal and glass doors make for memorable entrances, while the bar's machined metal fixtures and sleek lines create an austere urban style. And the dining room is flawlessly color-coordinated for autumn: copper columns, ochre walls, and woody accents. Even the lighting is designed for perfection; the amber hue could give the Wicked Witch of the West good skin tone.

Though the menu has European influences, Dixie-drawn dishes are in the spotlight. Starters include Gulf shrimp steeped in chardonnay, fried oysters with wasabi soy sauce, and lump fin crab cakes, which are plump, Old Bay-speckled egg shapes served with a biting Tabasco and jalapeño-chile dip. While in the seafood mood, sample the skillfully prepared Lowcountry crab and corn chowder, whose luscious texture comes from a plenitude of flaky white crab meat rather than too much cream.

Dinner is blackened catfish with mashed potatoes and greens, barbecue ribs, or cornmeal-dipped whiting with potato and onion strings and a brightly flavored dip of mayonnaise, red onion, dill, cayenne, and gherkins. The crisp-crusted smothered pork chops are made distinctive by oniony gravy and the accompaniment of scrumptious fried apples that could easily be dessert. But dessert is sweet potato pecan pie, in a nutty crust surrounded by a pool of syrupy pecan sauce and whipped cream.

B. Smith's is the rare pre-theater establishment offering comfort food with all the show of the Big City, and the service is appropriately swift. So if you're not off to see the Phantom or singing pussycats, tell your waiter up front...'cause they work it!

"THE FACT IS SIMPLY THAT FOR THE NORTH, THE SOUTH IS TOO THEATRICAL TO BE WHOLLY REAL; THEREFORE IT IS 'HISTORY' AND NOT 'REAL LIFE.'"
—RICHARD WEAVER,
SOUTHERN HISTORIAN & PHILOSOPHER

# CAFE BEULAH

∎∎∎∎∎∎∎∎∎∎∎∎∎∎∎∎∎∎∎∎∎∎∎∎∎∎∎∎∎∎∎

**39 E. 19TH STREET**
**BET. BROADWAY & PARK AVENUE SOUTH**
**212-777-9700**
**MAJOR CREDIT CARDS**

**MAIN COURSES: $16–$25**

U pon arrival at Cafe Beulah, a patchwork Southern past leaps to life through pictures. South Carolina native Alexander Smalls has created a living, breathing family album in his home-spun "Southern Revival" restaurant. Family photos are the focus of the decor, as proudly displayed as a Van Gogh because their cultural legacy is the reason for Beulah's being.

Beaulah's buttercup yellow, slat-wood wainscot-ing and cream-colored picture railing could so easily have been a backdrop in one of those photos. From the wrought iron Charleston-style front gate to the haint green accents and wood blinds, Beulah is stylistically perfect in its portrayal of South Carolina's Lowcountry. The soft sound of the blues, the whoosh of the ceiling fans, and the smooth mint juleps with shaved ice are neither hackneyed nor insincere; Mr. Smalls has creat-ed an oasis for wayward Southerners without any of that "Y'all come" bid'ness.

The menu is a sensory overload of dishes repre-senting Lowcountry cooking at its best, but with a gourmet twist. Hoppin' John, the New Year's good luck charm of rice and black-eyed peas, gets revamped; the same ingredients are mashed, heat-spiked, fried until crunchy, and then stacked and surrounded by swirls of honey mustard. Thick slices of duck pâté are served with cherry-pear chutney and what can only be described as wafer-thin biscuit bottoms. Humble chicken livers get gussied up with a flour-and-sage breading, sauteed greens, and an orange-mustard sauce. Or you may be fortunate enough to stumble upon specials such as creamy black-eyed pea and yam soup or crawdaddy hush puppies.

Some main courses steer clear of Southern influences, but Alexander's gumbo plate—seafood, sausage, duck, corn, and okra with red rice in Creole sauce—is right on the money. Ditto the slow-baked praline ham on a mound of garlicky greens and a sweet potato/green apple version of potato salad, all surrounded by a ring of berry-tinged bourbon sauce. Lowcountry fare is fluffy, herbed crawfish and sage sausage pilau or stick-to-your-ribs, pan-smothered shrimp and grits, an Esther Williams spectacle of seared prawns diving headfirst into a bowl of smooth hominy with wilted greens as a center raft.

The sepia-toned figures represent not just Smalls' ancestry, but the life-affirming memories of any transplanted Southerner fortunate enough to spend an evening here. Suddenly, "Southern Revival" is so appropriate; it's not just down-home cuisine being revived at Beulah, it's the essence of the Old South as a whole. Now you are dwelling in Beulah Land.

# CARMICHAEL'S DINER

▼▲▼▲▼▲▼▲▼▲▼▲▼▲▼▲▼▲▼▲▼▲▼▲▼▲▼

**117-08 GUY R. BREWER BLVD. AT FOCH BLVD.**
**JAMAICA, QUEENS**
**718-723-6908**
**CASH ONLY**

**MAIN COURSES: $6–$10**

oadside silver streak diners are nostalgic classics, famous for their retro decor, gum-smacking waitresses and, of course, grease-laden, quick-cooked fare that is uniquely American. But it's rare for one to be known as something totally different—a soul food haven. Presenting Carmichael's Diner...

A bus ride from Jamaica Center down Guy Brewer Boulevard finds you on the Carmichael clan's corner (their side-by-side enterprises include a gas station, liquor store, and travel agency), where the family's crown jewel eatery has stood for three decades. The interior is a kind of time capsule—endless counters with red vinyl stools, sun-streaked curtains surrounding train car windows, plastic-topped cake stands, and booths with individual wood-grained jukeboxes. Outside of a drop-ceilinged, add-on dining room in the rear, it seems nothing has been toyed with since their grand opening.

Sundays here are the stuff of local legend, where families in their Sunday best crowd in for good food and good company. The menu leans heavily toward breakfasts of salty, cured Smithfield ham, salmon patties, biscuits and grits with never ending cups of strong coffee. Lunch and dinner, on the other hand, begin with slow-steeped, amber iced tea (sugar stirred in, if you like, meaning it gets sweeter as you sip) and yellow cornbread so crumbly it disintegrates when touched. Enjoy it with a fork.

Carmichael's Southern-style meats are glorious, from the tender, chicken-fried pork chops to the cornmeal encrusted porgies, a bony but milky white fish. They arrive scorching from the fryer and crying out for splashes of hot sauce. A heaping helping of chopped barbecue is terrific as well, filled with red pepper flecks, a briny vinegar sauce, and the taste of the pit without ever being near one. And the well-fried chicken is outstanding in its field, a carefully wrought, tasty through-and-through version of the familial favorite.

Sides are hit-and-miss. Smoke-infused collards stand out as the best. The mac and cheese is creamy and smooth—it would make the Colonel proud. Sweet potato pie, "fresh daily" cakes, and lemon pie (with a seamlessly sculptured meringue and a flaky crust) melt quickly in any dessert-hungry mouth.

On Sundays, local congregations are Carmichael's regulars; they know better than anyone exactly what to order and how things work. Best advice on getting a great meal? Follow the lead of the church ladies.

# CAROLINA
# COUNTRY KITCHEN

▼▲▼▲▼▲▼▲▼▲▼▲▼▲▼▲▼▲▼▲▼▲▼▲▼

**1993 ATLANTIC AVENUE AT SARATOGA AVENUE**
**BEDFORD-STUYVESANT, BROOKLYN**
**718-346-4400**
**CASH ONLY**

**MAIN COURSES: $7–$9**

**P**lenty of New York restaurants transport Southern culture to the concrete jungle, but few do it like Carolina Country Kitchen. At the back of a wide parking lot is a pitched roof, wood-sided building resembling some kind of Kuntry Cookin' franchise in a Southern suburb. It's just like eating out in the South today: homemade meals in a jiffy at low, low prices.

The dining room, with its itsy-bitsy blue goose wallpaper, is a true-to-life version of a New South decorative trend best described as "exploding arts and crafts fair." It's all Mason jars, ribboned wreaths, and country crock scenes painted on saws and skillet bottoms. Alas, no quilted chickens.

Eclipsed by the zigzagging line of patrons is a steam table, where the daily deals are displayed. They don't sit for long, though; fresh pots of salty collard greens and field peas arrive constantly. On busy days, the women behind the counter dish it up like the dickens with minimal chitchat. No matter. Whatever you end up with is bound to be incredible. The chitlins and hog maws are a hard-to-find delicacy in these parts. Owner Patricia Lee has the chopped barbecue trucked in from North Carolina, so it is a fine, vinegary example of what pit-cooked pig is all about (it's porky perfection, so forego the extra sauce).

Lightly fried, thin-sliced pork chops smothered in tasty brown gravy are equally tempting, as are the pungent oxtails. Wide pans of bright-yellow macaroni pie, fresh off-the-cob corn, soupy green limas, and piquant okra and stewed tomatoes are only some of the distinguished additions. The golden-topped, white cornbread is perfect for sopping. And like Georgia kudzu, mile-high layer cakes and pies ranging from pecan—gooey with Karo syrup—to sweet potato, have taken over an unused grill.

Carolina Country Kitchen is a realistically modern Southern experience, as much for the Dollywood decor as the victuals. For suburbanites of the South (and those who love them), this is a sentimentally gustatory ride...replete with hay bales and wagon wheels. Really.

ACROSS THE STREET FROM CAROLINA COUNTRY KITCHEN IS ITS 30-YEAR-OLD SISTER, NORTH CAROLINA COUNTRY PRODUCTS (1991 ATLANTIC AVENUE, 718-498-8033). MS. LEE STOCKS THE STORE WITH HARD-TO-FIND SOUTHERN STAPLES THAT ARE SHIPPED UP FROM MAGNOLIA, NORTH CAROLINA ON A WEEKLY BASIS.

# CHANTALE'S
# CAJUN KITCHEN

**510 NINTH AVENUE**
**BET. 38TH & 39TH STREETS**
**212-967-2623**
**CASH ONLY**

**MAIN COURSES: $4–$7**

In 1994, a self-taught cook opened a storefront restaurant in the then relatively desolate area just south of the Port Authority. The result was a pint-sized cafe with a mishmash of influences: the flavors of Louisiana, a Caribbean-colored aura, and the ambiance of a beach shack. Though success for such eclecticism seemed improbable, Chantale's Cajun Kitchen was like The Little Engine That Could.

Chantale Bayard-Fabri has a vision. To keep things relaxed and simple, she offers counter-only service, plasticware and paper plates in colorful wicker holders. With her outgoing personality, she turns mere customers into regulars. She gladly describes the subtleties and ingredients of each dish. Chantale even gives directions to wandering tourists, and the brightly painted bench out front provides comfort for passersby in need of a short rest.

Chantale seals the deal by creating Cajun masterpieces, including chicken and sausage jambalaya and a variety of gumbos, all spiked with just enough cayenne to make the senses leap to attention. The gumbo bearing her name is a spicy cup of greatness, a brown-brothed assemblage of rice, celery, sausage, chicken, and seafood that would make the Soup Nazi blush. The milder, tomato-based Creole chicken, shrimp, or vegetables can be sampled with rice and black beans or as a sandwich on a thick slice of French country bread.

Then there are the daily specials (the same from week to week), hearty dishes like Cajun shepherd's pie and the peppery, sand dollar-sized crab cakes, with herb-flecked corn muffins and white rice drizzled with a spectacularly smooth cumin and bay leaf-flavored tomato sauce. Raisin and coconut-infused bread pudding from her grandmother's century-old recipe is the only dessert needed. The menu also has plenty of modern fare and vegetarian choices—Southern but healthy.

These days, the neighborhood is up-and-coming and the vision has paid off. Chantale's Cajun Kitchen is as busy as a fast-food joint without ever being anything less than a culinary marvel.

"CAJUN" IS A SHORTENED VERSION OF "ACADIAN," THE TERM ASCRIBED TO THE FOLKS OF ACADIA, THE REGION OF LOUISIANA KNOWN AS THE BIRTHPLACE OF GUMBO, COURTBOUILLON, AND MANY A GOOD ÉTOUFFÉE. THEIR ANCESTORS NEVER BLACKENED ANYTHING, THOUGH. THAT'S A NEW ORLEANS INVENTION DATING BACK TO...THE 1970S.

# CHARITY NEIGHBOR-
## HOOD AUXILIARY
### RESTAURANT

▪▪▪▪▪▪▪▪▪▪▪▪▪▪▪▪▪▪▪▪▪▪▪▪▪

**1515 BEDFORD AVENUE AT LINCOLN PLACE**
**PROSPECT HEIGHTS, BROOKLYN**
**718-773-9198**
**CASH ONLY**

**MAIN COURSES: $5–$7**

As anyone from a small Southern town knows, church tends to be the center of all life. It's where friends and family spend every Sunday, it's the fabric of the community, and it's where you're entertained because this is a podunk, one-horse burg with nothing to do except watch paint dry. So everyone gathers for picnics and covered dish dinners to socialize and chow down on the best Southern food around. What if those church ladies got together to open an eatery featuring their favorite dishes? That's Charity Neighborhood Auxiliary Restaurant, sans the sermon.

The corner locale, appropriately enough, feels like a church social hall—high tin ceilings painted industrial brown; beige tiled walls; speckled linoleum floors; red-and-white checkered tablecloths under plastic; nothing on the walls. It's no-nonsense, and so is the service. These ladies will sit with you to take your order, make suggestions, and send you off with "Have a blessed evening," but they take no gump.

Freshness is the key ingredient for good Southern cooking, and everything here is fresh, fresh, fresh. Cabbage is pungent and leafy, string beans snap with flavor, and sweet yellow turnips are mashed until creamy. Starchy sides are equally good, such as eggy potato salad with kelly-green flecks of pickle and white rice held together by a spoonful of thick chicken gravy. And the cornbread is right as rain and devoid of sugar, a fact that elicits a "Praise the Lord!" from anybody sick of New York's endless supply of cakey pone.

The ladies offer an amazingly wide variety of meats—lamb shank, pig's feet, oxtails, Cornish hens, beef brisket, fried fish—at rock-bottom prices. Charity's fried chicken is a surefire prizewinner, a masterfully prepared piece of poultry, and the rail-thin, well-done pork chops are almost as crunchy as pork rinds.

Cups of faultless cobbler are a fitting end to any Charity meal, with peaches or apples mixed into a cinnamon syrup and buttressed by flaky pastry bits. Just try skipping dessert and you'll get a raised eyebrow followed by, "You don't know what you're missing." When you need inspiration to make the trip to Charity, remember those wise words.

IF CHARITY LIFTS YOUR SPIRITS, CONSIDER READING SOUL FOOD: RECIPES AND REFLECTIONS FROM AFRICAN-AMERICAN CHURCHES. JOYCE WHITE SPENT YEARS VISITING HARLEM CHURCHES FOR FELLOWSHIP AND A TASTE OF HOME. THE RESULT WAS THIS COLLECTION OF REAL STORIES AND FABULOUS FOOD.

# Charles'
# Southern Style
# Kitchen

▪▪▪▪▪▪▪▪▪▪▪▪▪▪▪▪▪▪▪▪▪▪▪▪▪▪▪

**2839 Eighth Avenue**
**Bet. 151st & 152nd Streets**
**212-926-4313**
**Cash Only**

**Main Courses: $6–$7**

**B**low, Gabriel, blow. That's what the throngs of people waiting outside Charles' Southern Style Kitchen are waiting for. Even when the opening time for this tiny take-out counter is a mere 10 minutes away, no one paces or pushes. Everyone tries to get a look at what miracles are being performed behind the glass. Inside, Charles Gabriel, a 22-year veteran of the stalwart Copeland's, is creating a little slice of heaven.

Charles' culinary skills were once (and sometimes still are) a traveling salvation show, his catering truck roaming the streets of Harlem dispensing loving cups of chopped barbecue, pig's feet and fluffy rice with salty cowpeas. His following increased, word spread rapidly, and Charles opened a storefront to serve the gastronomic needs of a burgeoning and hungry congregation. Now he has expanded into a cafe next door.

A young woman speaks reverently of the smothered turkey wings and meatloaf, then gasps and points as she catches sight of brilliant yellow macaroni and cheese and, out of thin air, bubbling pork chops being raised from a larger-than-life iron skillet. Somebody gives testimony about the time they were blessed with an extra helping of the okra, tomato, and corn mix, and nearly speaks in tongues when describing the smothered pork chops, which are batter-fried and then blanketed in a beatific gravy.

Stories of Charles' legendary fried chicken circulate, with words like heat-sealed juiciness, flavor-packed, bodacious, sacrosanct, and be-all-end-all floating about like angels' wings. Everyone attests to its unsurpassed glory, and the resplendent fragrance suddenly makes its way past the locked door. They wonder how it is that Charles has not yet smote all by-the-bucket chicken chains. Charles' sweet potato pie and candied yams are hailed as miracles along with his hunks of chocolate layer cake.

Someone clamors for oxtails and greens right that very moment, threatening to break the peace. An old-timer smiles and reminds them, "The longer you wait, the better it'll taste." Everyone sighs and nods in agreement. A key turns, and Mr. Gabriel opens the pearly gates.

TO MOST, DUNCAN HINES IS SYNONYMOUS WITH CAKE MIXES, BUT THE REAL HINES WAS A SOUTHERNER AND FOOD CRITIC. IN THE '30S, THE KENTUCKIAN BEGAN TAKING NOTES ON EATERIES ENCOUNTERED IN HIS FREQUENT TRAVELS. HIS ADVENTURES IN GOOD EATING GUIDE WAS THE RESULT. IT WAS SO SUCCESSFUL, HINES WAS EVENTUALLY ASKED TO LEND HIS NAME TO A LINE OF HIGH-QUALITY FOODS.

# COOKING WITH JAZZ

**12-01 154TH STREET AT 12TH AVENUE**
**WHITESTONE, QUEENS**
**718-767-6979**
**VISA/MASTERCARD**

**MAIN COURSES: $12–$24**

After four years under the tutelage of Louisiana legacy Paul Prudhomme, Chef Steven Van Gelder returned home to Queens and set up business for himself. His restaurant, Cooking With Jazz, relies on kick-ass cuisine, attentive service, and a neighborhood warmth sparked by Van Gelder himself, acting most nights as host, waiter, culinary encyclopedia, and, of course, chef.

The restaurant is a hassle to get to from Manhattan (an hour by subway and bus), it's tiny (on weekends, patrons practically sit in each other's laps), and it has limited decor (chile lights and Mardi Gras masks). But Cooking With Jazz serves incredible Cajun, so you're in for an amazing experience.

A Cajun martini of jalapeño-flavored vodka and a basket of nutty muffins and peppery sourdough bread whet the appetite. For now, pass over the "Not So Cajun" side of the menu and begin with plump, barely-fried oysters, smoked alligator sausage, or fried and

SEA·FOOD
OUR SPECIALTY

stuffed eggplant, crisp slices with a fiery seafood corn-bread dressing in a buttercream shrimp sauce. Even ravioli makes a marvelous Acadian appetizer, filled with tasso and chopped shrimp and smothered in a tomato-cream sauce.

What Van Gelder does with Cajun basics puts most versions to shame. Étouffée eschews crawfish and rice for chicken and garlicky potatoes. Jambalaya becomes tasso rice, a greaseless, superbly blackened chicken breast, and a slab of andouille, all in a savory okra-tomato sauce. And barbecued shrimp, so often ruined by kitchens far and wide, are ten eye-popping, heads-on prawns sauteed in a glorious rosemary, pepper, and beer blend. They're insanely messy but worth every juice-splattered, finger-licking moment.

Dessert—with a cup of chicory-blend coffee—is a sensual experience. Medallions of banana flambéed in brown sugar and Grand Marnier with vanilla ice cream comprise the superlative bananas Foster. Bread pudding is a mountainous scoop of a cinnamon-infused, crumbly brown mélange. And though it's far from Southern, Van Gelder whips up a cheesecake so fluffy and fabulous it's a shoo-in for New York's best.

Satisfied to the point of bursting, jalapeño jelly beans in hand, and with the "Shalom, Y'all!" exit sign seared in your mind, thoughts of another journey begin before reaching the parking lot. The first time is a trek; returning is a labor of love.

# COPELAND'S

▗▖▗▖▗▖▗▖▗▖▗▖▗▖▗▖▗▖▗▖▗▖▗▖▗▖▗▖▗▖▗▖▗▖▗▖▗▖

**547 W. 145TH STREET**
**BET. BROADWAY & AMSTERDAM AVENUE**
**212-234-2357**
**MAJOR CREDIT CARDS**

**MAIN COURSES: $9–$23**

Since 1962, Calvin Copeland has quietly created an uptown phenomenon. What began as "reliable" catering evolved into Copeland's Reliable cafeteria. Eventually, an upscale second restaurant was opened next door to the original. Decades later, the double threat dynamic duo roll onward and upward.

One wildly busy kitchen serves both restaurants, but they're worlds apart. From the 145th Street subway stop, the cafeteria is first up, a glaring fluorescent vision from out front. It's an eat-and-run operation: burger joint seating, backlit menu board, quick-serve steam counter. Streams of diners wend their way in (hungry) and out (stuffed).

Reliable breakfasts are sizzled beef or pork sausage, toasty salmon croquettes, platter-sized griddle cakes, and grits. The sauteed and smothered chicken livers—inexplicably reserved for the wee hours—are exquisitely and copiously sauced. Dinners are also classic: awesome oxtails, smothered chicken and pig's feet, all with heaps of sides.

Harder to spot is the restaurant next door. Tinted windows mask a dark cocktail lounge and—beyond an odd arrangement of latticework and dried flowers springing from giant seashells—the more formal Copeland's. From beigey-gold wallpaper and tablecloths to deep-brown napkins, everything is awash in autumnal tones. At the back is a Wall of Fame, hung with paintings of black celebrities, while at the opposite end is a velvet-swathed backdrop where gospel groups perform at Sunday brunches. Best of all are the chandeliers, closely resembling Superman's Krypton crystal-keepers.

Unlike Reliable next door, Copeland's restaurant offers as much typical American fare as "Southern Kitchen" dishes. Slightly sweet biscuits start things off, along with Mississippi smoked catfish, a bowl of peanut soup, or chitterlings vinaigrette, a cold version of the famous (or infamous) soul specialty. Boiled chitlins are also a main course, steaming and served with champagne. Honest-to-goodness, pan-fried chicken with corn fritters is another fan favorite, as is the crisp and succulent fried catfish. And ever-present collards are beyond the pale; these are possibly the most beguiling, husky-flavored, and utterly superlative greens this city has to offer.

Copeland's is worthy of the legendary hoopla, and yet it's been lucky enough to elude the plague of touristy chaos. With that—and so much more—going for it, "reliable" is far too modest.

**BEYOND ALL THE GRIT-EATING GOING ON IN GOTHAM'S SOUTHERN RESTAURANTS, NEW YORK SUPERMARKETS SELL MORE THAN 2.2 MILLION POUNDS OF GRITS A YEAR.**

# COWGIRL
# HALL OF FAME

▪▪▪▪▪▪▪▪▪▪▪▪▪▪▪▪▪▪▪▪▪▪▪▪▪▪▪▪▪▪▪▪▪

**519 HUDSON STREET AT 10TH STREET**
**212-633-1133**
**MAJOR CREDIT CARDS**

**MAIN COURSES: $8–$17**

**W**hoa, Nellie! Forget Planet Hollywood and the Cafes (Fashion, Hard Rock, Motown, and whatever pops up next week) dishing out mediocrity on a platter. Cowgirl Hall of Fame is what a memorabilia-filled restaurant should be: celebrity worship and great food. Inspired by the museum of the same name founded in Hereford, Texas, and now located in Fort Worth, Cowgirl not only celebrates the height and breadth of Dale Evans' hairdo but also what she would probably want for chow after a day on the range.

Guzzle a Lone Star longneck in the Western kitsch of the bar, then browse through the General Store for items like plastic farm animals, Childhood Memory Candy (including lip-puckering Smarties and jaw-breaking Fireballs), and leather Cowgirl postcards fashioned as oversized blue jean patches.

Once seated in the dining room, which can best be described as Wagon Wheel Chic, replete with cactus sconces and rawhide lamp shades, it's time to start working your way through that ominously large stack of napkins on the table. Get the mess going with the

Frito Pie (smokin' beef or vegetarian Chuckwagon Chili, cheese, onions, and sour cream piled on the corn chips and served right in the bag) or a cube-shaped batch of lightly fried onion rings.

Bigger 'n Dallas entrees range from the good-as-Granny's chicken-fried chicken with creamy gravy and chunky mashed taters to cracker-crusted catfish with zesty jalapeño tartar sauce. And there are few better choices than the lip-smackingly good whiskey pork chops, which are chargrilled and smothered with a marmaladelike Jack Daniels glaze; they should be Cowgirl's claim to fame, but some still stampede in for the Tex-Mex. Go figure. Barbecued ribs or chicken dishes are a real feast and a house specialty, but sauce lovers will want to ask for extra dollops on the side.

Anyone longing for Texas is sure to love a place that can serve kid-friendly corn dogs and mount a Patsy Cline look-alike contest, all with a straight face. Cowgirl Hall of Fame is theme restaurant meets theme park meets trailer park. Happy trails.

FORT WORTH'S NATIONAL COWGIRL MUSEUM AND HALL OF FAME TAKES THE WOMEN OF THE WILD WEST QUITE SERIOUSLY. FROM DAREDEVIL RIDERS TO RANCHERS, NEARLY 150 HONOREES ARE CITED FOR THEIR "REAL LIFE GRIT." GIVE 'EM A HOLLER AT 817-336-GIRL.

# DEW DROP INN

▞▞▞▞▞▞▞▞▞▞▞▞▞▞▞▞▞▞▞▞▞▞▞▞

**57 GREENWICH AVENUE AT PERRY STREET**
**212-924-8055**
**MAJOR CREDIT CARDS**

**MAIN COURSES: $7–$11**

According to lore, the inspiration for Dew Drop Inn's cuisine came from a Route 66-style trip by the restaurant's owners. They apparently detoured into the Deep South, because the menu resembles something from a dust-blown roadhouse, grease-streaked and mouth-watering at the same time. You can almost see George Raft in a booth, having a cup of Joe and a slice of apple pie after driving all night.

But the final look is more post-modern, a Formica-filled vision in red, white, and blue with Deco accents. Lots of kidney shapes and glitter; imagine the Jetsons' space age house smashing into a truck stop, and you've got the picture. The background music is equally schizophrenic, moving wildly from Ella to Phish without warning.

Dew's appetizer section reads like the side panel of a Velveeta carton, careening into the realm of bar munchies. The best beginnings are found on the drink menu, an homage to Southern libations with names like Magnolia Blossom, Damn Shame, Plantation Peach Fuzz, and Fall Off the Porch Tea, with most including such Southern staples as Jack Daniels and Southern Comfort. The fun-loving staff will steer you right.

Appropriately enough, entrees arrive on faded oval platters that look as if they should bear the name of a long-forgotten, back-road cafeteria. And the same kind of food would have been served on them: slabs of chicken-fried steak with mild and milky sausage gravy, thick, white catfish, perfectly blackened or deep-fried to a crunch, or Dr Pepper chicken, a poultry quarter marinated in the sticky Dixie liquid and grilled until it's a trailer park delicacy to die for. Big mounds of traditional side dishes complete the homespun picture: brackish collards, fried potatoes, and ice-cold slaw and potato salad. And do have that slice of crumbly, deep-dish apple pie.

To best enjoy Dew Drop Inn, particularly on a rowdy summer night, grab a table outside. The conversation is easier, and the roadhouse cuisine can be savored in peace before you once again head out on that big, open highway.

WRITER JOHN EGERTON TOOK THE DEFINITIVE ROAD TRIP IN SEARCH OF THE BIBLE BELT'S BEST EATS BEGINNING IN 1984, THEN CHRONICLED IT ALL IN 1987'S INDISPENSABLE <u>SOUTHERN FOOD: AT HOME, ON THE ROAD, IN HISTORY</u>. HIS MEALS AT 335 RESTAURANTS IN 11 STATES TRANSLATE INTO FAR MORE THAN A GUIDE TO BABY BACKS AND BEIGNETS; IT IS A DETAIL-RICH HISTORY OF THE CULINARY RITUALS AND TRADITIONS OF THE SOUTH.

# DUKE'S

▪▪▪▪▪▪▪▪▪▪▪▪▪▪▪▪▪▪▪▪▪▪▪▪▪▪▪▪▪

**99 E. 19TH STREET**
**BET. PARK AVENUE SOUTH & IRVING PLACE**
**212-260-2922**
**MAJOR CREDIT CARDS**

**MAIN COURSES: $9–$15**

**D**uke's is high on the hog meets high camp. From its roadhouse bar plastered with vinyl 45s to its storefront-size neon sign spelling out L-I-Q-U-O-R, the riotous restaurant's approximation of redneck chic is an absolute hoot. In the case of this over-the-top, self-anointed potentate of potbellies, imitation really is the sincerest form of flattery.

The front room is often home to a bellowing after-work crowd that congregate around the filling station-style red Coke machine while swaying to the tunes of Peggy Lee. Beyond that lies a dining area rife with softly-lit Bible Belt charm: green vinyl booths, light shades the color of yellowed newspaper, and stark black-and-white photos chronicling the recent history of Southern

cuisine. It's as comfortable as any outpost below the Mason-Dixon line.

The menu is chock-full of regional specialties, including a Carolina pulled-pork sandwich, Chattanooga chili, and Louisiana jambalaya. There's catfish, including a fried or blackened version topped with a rock shrimp and mushroom ragout. Crab fritters are an irresistible start; scoops of deviled crab meat are battered, deep-fried, and served with a mayonnaisey remoulade sauce. Buttermilk-battered chicken with milk gravy is a good choice, but don't be misled by the menu's use of the words "chicken-fried." While it holds its own, it ain't chicken-fried.

Barbecue is king here, especially the Texas beef brisket with peppery tomato-based sauce and the slow-roasted dry-rub ribs (cooked all day in a big oven downstairs). Choose the mashed sweet potatoes and the excellent, smoky baked beans as accompaniments. For dessert, there's the daily fruit pie or Pensacola Coca-Cola cake, which utilizes the syrupy soda as a sweet tooth-pleasing part of its recipe.

As a souvenir of the Duke's experience, be sure to grab one of their collagelike menus on the way out. Recalling every one of the zillion Southern icons could give you a case of the vapors (start with easy ones, like the Piggly Wiggly oinker and the Sunbeam Bread girl). The folks at Duke's obviously thrive on Dixie kitsch, but it's their tag line that speaks volumes: "A Southern Dining Room." They're obviously proud to wear the label.

IN 1916, PIGGLY WIGGLY OPENED ITS FIRST LOCATION IN MEMPHIS, TENNESSEE. WHAT MADE IT DIFFERENT WAS THE FACT THAT PIGGLY WIGGLY WAS THE FIRST GROCERY STORE TO INTRODUCE SELF-SERVICE AND SHOPPING BASKETS. THEIR BIG IDEA CAUGHT ON. THEIR NAME, HOWEVER, TOOK SOME GETTING USED TO.

# EMILY'S

▰▰▰▰▰▰▰▰▰▰▰▰▰▰▰▰▰▰▰▰▰▰▰▰

1325 FIFTH AVENUE AT 111TH STREET
212-996-1212
MAJOR CREDIT CARDS

MAIN COURSES: $10–$18

**H**igh up Fifth Avenue, where Central Park comes to an end with rolling hills and a blaze of beauty, stands a statue of Duke Ellington and his piano. Like the moon over Dixie, Duke seems to be guarding the boogie-woogie homeland in addition to Emily's, the jazz-themed soul haven just across the way.

As another Harlem hipster, Cab Calloway, would have said, "Everybody eats when they come to this house." Emily's is all about food. The decor is simple, understated, and neat. With its sleek bar, soft-pink and yellow walls, music-maker portraits, and sun-colored swags of fabric trimming the floor-to-ceiling windows, this airy space is perfectly plain.

The menu's array of down-home dishes is as authentic as, in the words of Ellington, "magnolias dripping with honey." Sweet little squares of grainy cornbread and lemon-tinged iced tea start a taste bud tap dance, followed by a classic fried shrimp appetizer. The chopped pork barbecue is an ample portion of hickory-flavored goodness surrounded by toast points and richly red tomato slices; its baby back brother is also a meaty bet. Since whopping portions of both are available to take home (for that matter, most things come in quart-size containers to go), start thinking about your next meal before finishing this one.

If fried chicken is your standard unit of measure when considering the merits of country cooking, then Emily's easily earns itself a place in the pantheon of poultry. This moist, crisp-crusted, glistening gem makes hash of those fast-food phonies. Cornbread stuffing with robust giblet gravy and buttery, bubbling hot grits provide the perfect backup, with no pork products used as seasoning. The final touch is all-butter pound cake, thickly white-iced coconut layer cake, or rummy yum yum cake. All come in slices so big they'd push anybody over the edge.

To fully appreciate Emily's appeal, try it on for size during a Sunday gospel brunch or a weeknight featuring rhythm and blues or jazz. Might as well get your soul food fix—and a Swanee River Rhapsody, too.

**"RED BEANS AND RICELY YOURS,
LOUIS ARMSTRONG"**
(HIS CLOSING ON LETTERS)

# ETHEL'S SOUTHERN QUARTERS

▰▰▰▰▰▰▰▰▰▰▰▰▰▰▰▰▰▰▰▰▰▰▰▰▰▰

### 747 ST. NICHOLAS AVENUE
### BET. 147TH & 148TH STREETS
### 212-694-1686
### CASH ONLY

### MAIN COURSES: $6–$7

**E**thel wants you to eat. A lot. Like Mama fattening up the young-uns, this South Carolinian dishes up huge portions. Somehow you know not cleaning your plate would elicit a hands-on-hips stance and disapproving stares from the otherwise kindly-faced owner. And, by the way, it's Ms. Ethel.

About three steps away from the 145th Street subway stop is the odd room, a rectangle divided into a narrow passageway, a little bitty kitchen and a red-tiled dining area that, with luck, could hold 20 people (since Ethel does mainly takeout, seats are usually available).

Start with a glass of Ethel's dark, sweetened iced tea. Deviled eggs are 'bout the only appetizer, but you don't really need them with the mountains of food you're about to get. For a, ahem, light lunch, Ethel puts specialties on sandwiches, such as a boneless fried chicken or her own special meatloaf. There's also a salmon-cake burger.

And these are serious salmon cakes, so serious they're served at all three meals of the day. The inch-thick patties are deep-fried until rusty brown, and inside is a smooth mixture of onions, peppers, and flaky canned salmon (as it should be for the genuine soul food article). Lusty oxtails are another special-ty; tearing into these strongly flavored joints is a labor intensive but rewarding prospect.

Dinners come with fragile slivers of orangish-brown cornbread and two bountiful heaps of sides. The yams are best, quartered and sprinkled with just enough sugar and spice and everything nice. Other extraordinary choices are potato salad—composed of finely diced spuds, chunks of boiled egg, and sweet pickles—and the cheesy macaroni pie, soft and salty in the middle and crunchy around the edges. The collard greens, steamy and slow-stewed, have a preponderance of stems. In the end, there are those layer cakes loom-ing in the plastic stands or banana pudding—for those who can handle it.

Ethel, hidden in her kitchen domain, works her magic like the Wizard of Oz behind the curtain. You never know what may pop out of that bag of tricks; she makes what she wants when she wants, and when it's gone, it's gone. As the menu clearly states, "Some din-ner meats will not be prepared daily." Get there early and, if you know what's good for you, be hungry.

# GRANVILLE

━━━━━━━━━━━━━━━━━━━━━━━━━━━

**40 E. 20TH STREET**
**BET. BROADWAY AND PARK AVENUE SOUTH**
**212-253-9088**
**MAJOR CREDIT CARDS**

**MAIN COURSES: $17–$25**

From the front window of the restaurant, a corpulent and aloof Big Daddy character stares out dourly at all who enter the cigar bar/Creole domain. This oil painting and its forever frozen-in-time subject provide a perfect peek into what Granville is all about—the bygone, Southern Gothic opulence of the Crescent City come to conquer Manhattan.

The space is pure Tennessee Williams. Upstairs is the clubby cigar bar, a sanctuary of overstuffed leather furniture, flickering oil lights and cognac-scented air. Downstairs is the intimate dining room, a menagerie of boudoir lamps and banquettes. Lining the room are scrolled metal and mother-of-pearl wall sconces with a pseudoskylight to match. French Quarter-style black iron ceiling fans whirl methodically, propelled by creaking leather belts and pulleys. With its warm lighting, red-wine walls, and rich woods, the room extends a glowing kindness to strangers.

Chef Larkin Selman, an eighth-generation New Orleanian, created a "modern American Creole" menu for Granville that's spiced to perfection from beginning to end. Spring rolls take on new life as Bayou rolls with a spicy pear dip. Flaky, crisp-crusted Avery Island crab and crawfish cakes are drizzled with the flavors of summer and smoke in a jalapeño Tabasco aïoli. Creole salad is a finely chopped, lightly dressed mixture of greens, olives, red peppers, and bacon on paper-thin beet slices, topped with toasted pecan halves.

Filet mignon with stewed okra and Cajun roasted chicken are two superb entree choices; so is the cornmeal and chipotle-coated catfish, surrounded by a pungent herb aïoli and propped up on a mass of cowpeas and purple cabbage-carrot slaw. But the standout is spectacular sauteed tilapia: two cylindrical fish fillets,

golden brown and buttery from the pan, covered with crawdad tails, abutted by chile-infused corn macque choux, and blanketed in a robust shrimp bisque.

Follow-ups are fitting: they include a fresh-fig and praline napoleon with lemon port glaze and a coal-black Mississippi mud brownie with sinful peanut butter ice cream, sour-cherry chocolate sauce, and a sculpted, sweet bird of caramelized sugar perched atop the edifice. Finally, sink into an icy, ultrasmooth ginger mint julep. Perhaps if the Big Daddy mascot had sipped one before he sat for his portrait, he'd be greeting Granville's patrons with a toothy grin.

# GREAT JONES CAFE

▀▄▀▄▀▄▀▄▀▄▀▄▀▄▀▄▀▄▀▄▀▄▀▄▀▄▀▄▀▄▀▄

**54 GREAT JONES STREET**
**BET. BOWERY & LAFAYETTE STREET**
**212-674-9304**
**CASH ONLY**

**MAIN COURSES: $10–$13**

Great Jones Cafe conjures up images of a con-
verted filling station out on some steaming,
two-lane Louisiana highway; a utilitarian
structure that has passed hands a dozen times before ending up a roadside pit stop. With its cinder block-style
building painted the color of Orange Crush, creaky
screen door, and window-unit air conditioners, Great
Jones has a lot in common with those gas station odd-
balls. Yet this is far more than a wannabe dive smack dab
in the middle of the East Village. Great Jones is an
appealingly plainspoken neighborhood hangout that
knows what it can do and does it well.

Inside, it's pure East Village retro. Mardi Gras
beads are slung across light fixtures. Mummified baby
gators, a ceramic Madonna, and bowling pins are
proudly displayed behind the bar. Bubble gum tunes
fill the air. Beyond this semi-kitsch, furnishings are
bare bones: a few tables and chairs scattered about.

The entrees change daily, but a permanent menu is
painted on one long, white wall: burgers, baskets of sweet
potato or home-cut fries, chili of the day, and jalapeño
cornbread, which is a wedge of honey/chile drizzled
manna that is Jones' biggest bargain on any night.

Mighty Louisiana rules the roost, so count on seafood and spice. The hot appetizer to hope for is the succulent, beer-battered plate of jumbo shrimp with a heat-filled tartar sauce reminiscent of remoulade. Super-fiery shrimp, scallions, peppers, and andouille sausage are suspended in a thick brown gravy for Jones' take on filé gumbo. The same ingredients show up milder, drier, and mixed with sticky white rice in the hearty comfort food casserole, ya ya jambalaya. Both are robust versions of bayou basics. The Cajun meatloaf, though, is a simple, gravy-covered slice of home that's wonderfully plain-Jane but as Cajun as a tuna casserole.

Dessert is primarily pie, be it Key lime or chocolate pecan. Others could be recipes right out of *Ladies' Home Journal*. Witness the fluffy peanut-butter pie with its chocolate syrup and vanilla crust; it's a fun flashback that gets a fancy schmancy presentation, Martha Stewart-style.

With its ever-changing Cajun and wide range of regulars, Great Jones Cafe is forever evolving. On one of those bayou backroads, it would fit in just fine.

# THE HOG PIT

22 NINTH AVENUE AT 13TH STREET
212-604-0092
MAJOR CREDIT CARDS

MAIN COURSES: $11–$13

A dilapidated, pie-shaped red building at the edge of the meat packing district is home to a raucous barbecue joint, The Hog Pit. Like its infamous, rootin'-tootin' cousin, Hogs & Heifers saloon, The Hog Pit is frequented by stroller pushers to Chelsea boys, Hell's Angels to Hollywood royalty.

Playing on its name's double meaning, The Hog Pit mixes pigs (pork) and hogs (Harley Davidsons) in its biker bar/redneck dive decor. The Pit's "style" consists of "piggy" twinkle lights, Budweiser mirrors, steer skulls, and watchful wild boars' heads, each mounted above a motorcycle tank. There's a rifle above the bar (mercifully layered with thick dust) and a beaming belle in her shortest Daisy Dukes pouring the drinks. At the wide tables, condiments are organized in Corona six-pack cartons atop checkered-plastic coverings. A country and rockabilly jukebox and the occasional popping of a deep fryer set the mood.

Not ones to mess around, the Pit bosses offer up a slim selection of Southern standards and eschew an everything-but-the-kitchen sink menu. Besides the daily specials, the kitchen serves only pan-fried chicken (evenly battered, crispy little pieces that are incredibly close to Ma's), homemade meatloaf, fried catfish, and slabs of baby back ribs draped in a tart 'n' toma-toey, spicy 'n' sour barbecue sauce. These dishes come with two sides, most notably the mellow, all-white macaroni and cheese, creamed corn sliced right off the cob, and the onion-filled, sugary baked beans. And this may be the only place in town where you can bite into rattlesnake once a year.

Even more inviting are the half-dozen appetizers and desserts. Start dinner with hush puppies, a bowl o' chili, a basket of fast-fried green tomato slices, or the delicious fried pickles, which are dills smothered in a dense flour batter and deep-fried. Amazing—when available. Or open wide for the unabashedly trashy pea salad, a trailer toss of iceberg lettuce, baby peas, carrots, and bacon bits in a secret sauce. Dessert is simply coconut pie or banana pudding. Either will suffice, but Dykes on Bikes purportedly start the occasional brawl over soup bowls full of the custardy banana concoction.

Urban hipness is inching its way into this district which, until recently, was home only to the meat-pack-ing industry and other fleshy enterprises. The Hog Pit is seedy enough to fit right into the old neighborhood and cool enough to transcend it. Hop up high on the hog, baby, and get ready for the ride.

# JUSTIN'S

▪▪▪▪▪▪▪▪▪▪▪▪▪▪▪▪▪▪▪▪▪▪▪▪▪▪▪▪▪▪

**31 W. 21ST STREET**
**BET. FIFTH & SIXTH AVENUES**
**212-352-0599**
**MAJOR CREDIT CARDS**

**MAIN COURSES: $16–$27**

**D**ayumn! When gangsta rapper Sean "Puffy" Combs puts his mark on something, he doesn't mess around. The wunderkind is already working 24/7 as a musician, record-label owner, and, now, restaurateur with the ultraslick Justin's.

The high-ceilinged room is an exercise in subtlety. A toasty, golden glow flickers across waxed, blond wood floors and abstract paintings. Neutral glazed walls, smooth columns, and softly brushed metalwork abound. Everything from the enormous, semicircular booths to the Alice in Wonderland settees are in natural, earthy tones.

The menu ends the restraint with its dive into sinful soul. Puffy hired two extraordinary chefs: North Carolina native Denise Bonds and Marvin James, formerly of Gage & Tollner. They take something as basic as a chicken wing and make it sing. These chubby nibbles are triply blessed with deep-frying, honey-sweet barbecue sauce and blue-cheese dip, served in a mini homeskillet.

Bread baskets arrive overflowing with biscuits, cornbread slabs, and jam, followed by appetizers such as the pan-browned crab cake with tasty mustard slaw on one side and a bird's nest of shredded and fried sweet potatoes on the other.

Selections range from deep-fried chicken and smothered pork chops to bread crumb-coated Carolina catfish to the "Geechie specialty" of garlicky shrimp, inspired by the African-American "Gullahs" of the South Carolina and Georgia sea islands. And the cheese grits are so smooth Southerners will be convinced Justin's has a Yankee-free kitchen. Oven-braised short ribs of beef are fall-off-the-bone fabulous and draped in an apple-filled brown gravy. Triangular pieces of fried porgy (a saltwater bream) are hardcore fish camp fare, and that is definitely a compliment.

Main courses come with gargantuan scoops of crumbly, sharp Cheddar macaroni pie, buttery boiled cabbage or Thanksgiving-flavored yams, blended with golden raisins and without copious amounts of sugar. Red velvet cake, that tough-to-make Southern favorite, is the real McCoy; small, round layers are held together by loads of vanilla icing and complemented with a citrusy berry sauce and a chilly scoop of banana ice cream.

Justin's is named for Puff Daddy's son, and the menu is inspired by the dinner table legacy of his South Carolina grandmother. It's only natural, then, that this Southern outpost should be so big-family warm.

# KRISPY KREME

**38 E. 8TH STREET**
**BET. UNIVERSITY PLACE & BROADWAY**
**212-529-5111**

**265 W. 23RD STREET**
**BET. SEVENTH & EIGHTH AVENUES**
**212-620-0111**

**2 PENN PLAZA, 34TH STREET AT PENN STATION**
**212-947-7175**

**141 W. 72ND STREET, BET. COLUMBUS & BROADWAY**
**212-724-1100**

**280 W. 125TH STREET AT EIGHTH AVENUE**
**212-531-0111**

**CASH ONLY**

**MAIN COURSES: 65¢ AND 75¢**

"Hot Doughnuts Now" or "H.D.N." to hardcore Deep Southerners. That phrase has probably caused more traffic tie-ups than any other ever spoken or read below the Mason-Dixon line. When Southern drivers spot those words in blazing red-and-green neon, they know they'd be plumb crazy to pass 'em by. U-turns, horn blowing, and pedal-to-the-metal impatience are acceptable in the South's pursuit of one thing: warm, wet Krispy Kreme doughnuts.

Though the folks down yonder have been scarfing down those coveted, dewy K.K.s and getting D.W.I.s (Driving While Insulin-shocked) for 60 years, New Yorkers got their first chance at the sugar-coated wonders in 1996. Customers at the Chelsea operation went hog-wild, creating word-of-mouth popularity and pandemonium. Demand for the glossy little puffs instantly went through the roof. Now city slickers can feed continuously at five locations. But it's still not enough.

What is this force of nature that has held Southerners in its spell for so long and now seems poised to take over the world? Krispy Kreme started as a humble yeast-raised, slickly glazed pastry sold out of a stand in Salem, North Carolina. Before long, 14 varieties were popping out of arch roofed, Christmas-colored storefronts across the Deep South. They appealed to the region's collective sweet tooth and soon many Dixielanders were referring to doughnuts as "Krispy Kremes" in the same way they called all soft drinks "Co-Cola."

Now Krispy Kreme takes Manhattan. Their chaotic stores' glistening doughnut displays are secondary to the main attraction: a glass-enclosed conveyor belt where you can watch the secret-recipe goodies being shot out by their patented Ring King, drenched in a coat of sugary gloss and, if appropriate, iced or hand-filled with squirts of chocolate, jelly, lemon, cream, or custard. Crunchier crullers make it through as well, but it's those plain ol' glazed K.K.s that make most swoon.

This is truly easy eating, with an air-light doughnut for each hand barely lasting past your first sip of rich coffee. They seem capable, literally, of being inhaled. Don't try that with a bagel.

# LITTLE JEZEBEL
# PLANTATION

▼▲▼▲▼▲▼▲▼▲▼▲▼▲▼▲▼▲▼▲▼▲▼▲▼

**529 COLUMBUS AVENUE AT 86TH STREET**
**212-579-4952**
**AMERICAN EXPRESS**

**MAIN COURSES: $12–$15**

Little Jezebel Plantation reconstructs a long-vanished, antebellum world, from its distinctive cuisine to its genteel decor. Instead of falling prey to Old South clichés, this refined cafe serves no-nonsense plantation victuals in a soft, soothing atmosphere straight out of South Carolina's Lowcountry—Charleston on Columbus.

Spawned from its Midtown Mama, Jezebel, Little Jezebel serves basically the same menu at a more down-home price and in a casual atmosphere. Pale-green woodwork, slow-turning ceiling fans, crisp linens and lace, wrought-iron chairs, and hordes of lilies and tropical plants all make the dining room feel like a serene Savannah garden. Antique botanical prints, Roseville pottery, and stacks upon stacks of china (that are actually used) complete the mood. Note the juxtaposition of an ornate chandelier above a steam table, like some country club buffet.

The menu reads like the oldest in-print Junior League cookbook, Charleston Receipts: oxtails, fish chowder, and classic chicken and waffles. It can take a while to narrow your choices, so pass the time with honest-to-goodness buttermilk biscuits. The next step is a richly satisfying order of crispy chicken livers in a biting brown sauce or tangy rib tips. Or sample the Charleston she-crab soup, rife with the traditional flavors of mace and heavy cream, but enhanced by a sprinkle of cayenne.

Southern specialties include fried chicken in gravy and Carolina shrimp Creole. It's an "old family recipe" with slivered onions, peppers, celery, tomatoes and opaline shrimp on rice. Seafood Creole adds a bonus of lobster, mussels, and scallops. Baked spare ribs and short ribs are also promising choices, as is the ham in an orange, raisin, and wine sauce.

Cooked-all-day black-eyed peas and scoops of golden macaroni and cheese are excellent, and any Southern fanatic must try Little Jezebel's marvelous sauteed okra; it sheds new light on the pod of the gods. The grand finale can be pecan, lemon, or sweet potato-coconut pie. Kudos go to the Southern pecan rum cake: two slices of all-butter pound cake crusted with nuts and drenched in rum.

Little Jezebel is the perfect way to sample Big Jezebel's cuisine without the hustle and bustle surrounding the Theater District flagship, though she can be as plantation-pricey as her ancestor if you load up on the frills. Otherwise, this is a sanctuary of Southern charm far north of the Mason-Dixon line.

# LOUISIANA COMMUNITY BAR & GRILL

▪▪▪▪▪▪▪▪▪▪▪▪▪▪▪▪▪▪▪▪▪▪▪▪▪▪▪▪▪▪▪

**622 BROADWAY**
**BET. BLEECKER & HOUSTON STREETS**
**212-460-9633**
**MAJOR CREDIT CARDS**

**MAIN COURSES: $14–$21**

**M**anhattan's biggest clump of Cajun and Creole eateries is inexplicably angled between Houston and Lafayette. Texans and Louisianans could probably find a joke in there somewhere.

One of those restaurants, Louisiana Community Bar & Grill, seems to get the joke while whipping up Cajun that is no laughing matter. It is known for being a frozen-cocktail-drinking, peanut-munching, after-work scene, and a peek inside reveals what looks like one big bar area.

Behind the bottlenecked bar and stage set-up, though, is a peaceful clapboard dining room with belt-and-pulley ceiling fans, crawdaddy wall sconces, and a shotgun-blasted Jax beer sign...a quiet world unto itself. This was once the Manhattan branch of chef Paul Prudhomme's famous K. Paul's before it morphed into what is still a very good place to eat.

Prudhomme-inspired cooking makes up the bulk of the menu, so anybody on the prowl for mudbugs (a.k.a. crawfish, crayfish, crawdaddies) will not be disappointed. Meals begin with a heaping basket of yeasty jalapeño rolls and ginger muffins. Appetizers include buckets of crawfish (in season), red beans and rice with andouille sausage, and wicked alligator fritters: sweet gator tail fried up as a piquant, crunchy morsel atop splayed barbecue sauce and hot mustard.

Seafood dominates the entrees: blackened tuna, bronzed catfish, and shrimp feliza, a dish with Cajun seasonings and red pepper vinaigrette. The Creole standard, crawfish étouffée, is downright decadent. Its drawn butter and fish stock sauce is a smooth sensation smothering mounds of scallions, rice, and those tasty pink mini-lobsters. The seafood okra gumbo is chocked with a variety of fish, and it is not quite as taste bud-blistering as one might expect; a cup of it is the cost equivalent of the Louisiana Purchase. Chocolate dream or coconut cakes round off the meal, but homesick Southerners go for the custardy, vanilla wafer-crusted banana betty, which rivals the best picnic puddings.

For those craving a Dixie beer and Sleepy LaBeef singing the blues, Louisiana Bar & Grill's reputation is well-earned. For those seeking bayou cuisine, there's a surprise waiting just beyond the bar.

FIVE BLOCKS DOWN FROM L.C.B.&G., WHERE DIXIE BEER IS CHUGGED, THE SOUTHERN STANDARD "DIXIE" MADE ITS DEBUT AS PART OF A MINSTREL SHOW. IT WAS A HIT WITH NEW YORKERS, BELIEVE IT OR NOT, BEFORE BECOMING A CONFEDERATE ANTHEM.

# M & G DINER

▀▀▀▀▀▀▀▀▀▀▀▀▀▀▀▀▀▀▀▀▀▀▀▀▀▀▀▀

383 W. 125TH STREET AT MORNINGSIDE AVENUE

212-864-7326

CASH ONLY

MAIN COURSES: $9–$15

While Harlem's main drag, 125th Street, gets a corporate makeover, neighborhood fixtures like M&G Diner not only hang on but continue to thrive. After more than three decades of dishing up unbeatable soul food 24 hours a day, seven days a week, M&G still packs them in. Between regulars anchored to barstools, visiting preachers, and Columbia students, it's usually "full up."

In part, that's because the place is impossible to miss. It stands out like a neon billboard, with multicolored signs resembling a state fair. Declarations such as "Old Fashion But Good," "Soul Food," and "Southern Fried Chicken" beckon hungry passersby to stop dead in their tracks. Once inside, the jukebox provides a lasting first impression as gospel divas, blues masters, and Detroit's finest rip the room. A few tables are shoved against the fake wood paneling, but the focus is a narrow '50s counter, where hair-netted, polyester-uniformed waitresses cluster behind cake stands, chatting furiously. And more signs abound, announcing everything from breakfast hours to specials.

M&G's soul is just plain good. Fried chicken is indeed the house specialty; poultry quarters are dredged in flour, peppered, and pan-fried until picnic perfect. Ditto the brown-crisped pork chops, but in a larger portion. Other "meat and two" mainstays include baked ham, barbecued ribs, fried whiting, and a hearty, ketchup-topped meatloaf that would merit the Good Housekeeping Seal of Approval. And M&G has those hard-to-find chitlins, if you're so inclined. In keeping with soul tradition, the meats double as sandwiches.

Your choices of "two" range from juicy, baked macaroni and cheese to starchy, slow-cooked lima beans to bright orange yams so syrupy and cinnamon-filled they could be dessert. Speaking of which, the rotating varieties of desserts are homemade and no-frills fabulous. Try a hunk of caramel pound cake or lemon meringue pie, a custardy, real meringue-topped wonder in a well-baked, flaky crust.

Happen by at the crack of dawn, and a breakfast of crunchy salmon croquettes and grits or eternally popular chicken and waffles can be yours for around the cost of a Starbucks latte. At M&G, soul-bred goodness comes properly priced and fancy doesn't fly. The nth generation photocopied menu proclaims "Serving Soul Food is Our Business." You bet it is.

"I GREW UP EATING WELL. CHEESE GRITS, HOMEMADE BISCUITS SMOTHERED IN BUTTER, HOME-CURED HAM, RED-EYED GRAVY—AND THAT WAS JUST BREAKFAST."
—OPRAH WINFREY

# MEKKA

**▀▀▀▀▀▀▀▀▀▀▀▀▀▀▀▀▀▀▀▀▀▀▀▀▀▀▀▀▀▀▀▀▀▀**

**14 AVENUE A
BET. HOUSTON & 2ND STREETS
212-475-8500
MAJOR CREDIT CARDS**

**MAIN COURSES: $11–$15**

**T**hough not exactly the quasi-religious experience its name implies, Mekka certainly attracts devoted flocks with its promise of "soul kulture." That kulture is one of funk and fusion, an effusive staff, and authentic yet healthier-than-home cooking.

Like its uptown soul sister, Shark Bar, Mekka is decorated to the hilt, but in an ethereal and exotic way. Candles and color-corrected bulbs provide mystical mood lighting while polished metal accents—including a riveted wall that could be part of an airplane hangar—bounce flickering reflections across the room. Paprika-colored wallpaper, vivid-blue banquettes with primer gray vinyl cushions, and black acoustic-tiled ceilings finish off the clubby East Village meets Global Village ambiance.

Yet the menu is entirely Southern. Promising starters include Cajun grilled shrimp and chicken wings, served barbecued or Southern fried with Mekka's own hot sauce. Perhaps the most creative appetizer is the Soul Roll, a patchwork of sauteed chicken, collards, cowpeas, and rice encased in puff pastry and served with gravy for dipping—sort of a Southland empanada.

Main courses arrive on muted, three-compartment plates that conjure up memories of childhood days in school cafeterias—with far superior food, of course. The cornmeal-crusted Georgia farm-raised catfish is a flaky, snow-white fillet that, when coupled with two tangy sauces, becomes absolutely stellar. Forego the Southern stand-bys like chicken and ribs, and go for juicy cuts of blackened sirloin steak.

Choose celestial sides like mashed potatoes with Cheddar cheese blended in, pungent and hearty seasoned rice, or mind-altering candied yams, with the aromatic incense of cloves and cinnamon. Most of Mekka's vegetables are ever-so-slightly sweetened and flavored by the touch of smoked turkey, making for wonderfully offbeat collards, string beans, and black-eyed peas. Finally, cobbler with cling peaches, cinnamon-baked crust and a scoop of vanilla ice cream is the way to go for dessert. By the way, read the small-print provisions at the bottom of the menu concerning gratuities and sharing entrees before you order.

Mekka is a haven on Earth for the weary Southern-lover. And it is a place where all may find soul anew.

# MISS MAMIE'S
# SPOONBREAD TOO

▼▲▼▲▼▲▼▲▼▲▼▲▼▲▼▲▼▲▼▲▼▲▼▲▼▲▼

**366 W. 110TH STREET**
**BET. COLUMBUS & MANHATTAN AVENUES**
**212-865-6744**
**CASH ONLY**

**MAIN COURSES: $8–$10**

**D**oes Norma Jean Darden ever sit still? First, she was a model and actress. Then she teamed up with her sister Carole for the cookbook/family memoir *Spoonbread and Strawberry Wine*, which Darden adapted into a one-woman show. Next came another sisterly partnership, Spoonbread Catering, which brings country corn pudding and barbecued ribs to chic soirées. Now there's Miss Mamie's Spoonbread Too, a down-home cafe-cum-takeout place next door to their catering company.

Named for their late mother, the siblings' home cooking tribute would make any parent proud. The space is as instantly welcoming as grandma's kitchen, and the butter-yellow and forest-green dinette sets are arranged on a Southern-size scale (plenty of elbow room). Hazy family photos hang above sky-blue wainscoting, with kitchen utensils and cast-iron pans covering the back wall. And from cafe curtains to painted tins to red-and-white stenciled floors, a strawberry motif abounds.

Step up to the clay tile counter to place orders for

Darden's Southern Revival dishes, old favorites with spicy twists. Nutmeg, mustard, and garlic rev up superior fried chicken, served alone or draped in a distinctive brown gravy. Potato salad with apple-cider vinegar and loads of paprika transcends the mayonnaisey versions found elsewhere. Macaroni and cheese is al dente, with each mini elbow coated in sharp, glossy Cheddar and flecks of black pepper. Collard greens are a coarsely chopped wonder, smoky sweet and with a familiar vinegar twang. Even the high-as-a-cat's-back squares of cornbread get a dose of distinctiveness, with bits of jalapeño popping up here and there. And yes, they do serve spoonbread, a rustic cornmeal concoction that's oven browned on the edges and fluffy in the middle.

Fall-off-the-bone short ribs of beef are simple and classically perfect. Dark brown with crispy edges on the outside and deep pink on the inside, this massive cut is as tasty as any long-cooked, Sunday dinner pot roast. Speaking of traditional Southern offerings, Spoonbread whips up what has to be one of the smoothest, flakiest, most fragrant and citrusy sweet potato pies this city knows.

Model. Performer. Caterer. Family historian. Now successful restaurateur. Darden lets nothing languish on the back burner; she's got every iron skillet on the fire.

# MONCKS CORNER

**644 NINTH AVENUE**
**BET. 45TH & 46TH STREETS**
**212-397-1117**
**CASH ONLY**

**MAIN COURSES: $7–$9**

In the Lowcountry of South Carolina is a hamlet of 6,000, Moncks Corner. Its chief claim to fame is Mepkin Abbey, home to Cistercian-Trappist monks. Mepkin is located on a former rice plantation purchased by Manhattan magazine entrepreneur Henry Luce and wife Clare Boothe Luce (author of the New York high society catfight, *The Women*) in 1936, long after its heyday. They donated a portion of the land to the brotherhood for use as a monastery/egg farm in 1949. This Gotham couple gave the Moncks Corner township a retreat for the soul. Now Moncks Corner provides New York with a soulful retreat. It's a more than fair trade.

Moncks is a busy take-out and delivery place with a *take-out* single table for four and a Mayberry-friendly staff. The tiny, lemon-colored space overflows with linen and lace, *Playbills*, vintage album covers tacked to the walls, and mixed media art by locals. It's all inviting enough to make grabbing the only seats and sitting a spell worthwhile.

Moncks serves New Yorkers a combination of South Carolina Lowcountry and soul, with dishes ranging from specials like catfish and collards to fried shrimp and scallops with white rice. Vanilla-laced corn muffins can quell the hunger as you wait for your meat-and-two, but filling up on them would be a waste of space. Instead, hold out for the dizzying array of big-portioned, well-seasoned treats. The four-piece order of fried chicken comes either plain, smothered in an earthy gravy and falling off the bone, or coated in a General Tso-like honey sauce. Ruddy ham slices in a fine raisin sauce taste like a Thanksgiving pie smells; it's slow-cured comfort food. The shrimp Creole fuses prawns with piquant tomatoes and scallions on a bed of rice.

Every item at Moncks is deliciously tweaked, particularly the accompanying sides: macaroni and cheese is dense and Cheddary with a touch of fieriness; okra slices are vinegar-tinged and sauteed; spicy, robust collards leave a lip-tingling wake; and the intact sweet potatoes are loaded with cinnamon, not sugar. For a sampling, the vegetarian platter will do you just fine.

Caramel-brown sweet potato pie and banana pudding make for soothing smalltown desserts. Perfect way to end a visit to idyllic Moncks Corner.

"IF YOU THROW A LAMB CHOP INTO A HOT OVEN, WHAT'S GONNA KEEP IT FROM GETTIN' DONE?"
—JOAN CRAWFORD TO BUTTERFLY MCQUEEN IN CLARE BOOTHE LUCE'S THE WOMEN

# Mr. Leo's Southern Cuisine

━━━━━━━━━━━━━━━━━━━━━━━━━━

**17 W. 27th Street**
**Bet. Fifth Avenue & Broadway**
**212-532-6673**
**Major Credit Cards**

**Main Courses: $10–$19**

**P**added, white vinyl banquettes. Mirrored walls. Pink-and-gold lighting. Enormous plastic flower arrangements. No, this isn't the set for a Doris Day movie, circa 1962. It's Mr. Leo's Southern Cuisine, a delightfully bizarre establishment that has been serving up splendid Southern feasts for over 15 years.

Once you've had some time to soak in the atmosphere, start your perusal of the enormous menu (so huge it takes up half the table when splayed out). The

selections and combos are mind-bogglingly extensive. If you're timing is right, you'll hit upon Leo's bargain-priced, all-inclusive lunch specials, one of the best deals in town.

Glasses of artificially lemon-flavored iced tea arrive in tropical drink glassware. That's followed up by creamy, delectable collard green soup and lightly sweetened, yellow corn bread sticks that will put anyone on the road to total relaxation. Go ahead. Sink back into those banquettes (they're really quite comfy).

There are still more decisions to be made. Will it be the Georgia honey-dipped fried chicken, the pork chops smothered in good-as-Mama's gravy, or the $33 barbecue combo of short ribs, chicken, pork, and shrimp (a kind of Pig-Out Pu Pu Platter)? Perhaps the chitterlings and pig's feet with a complimentary glass of champagne? How to choose between the shiny, sharp Cheddar macaroni and cheese, the fluffy mashed potatoes, and the exquisite vinegar-and-fatback-laced greens? What about the highly tempting battered and golden-fried versions of every meat, poultry, and seafood known to man and Southerner? Not to worry. Any selection from the authentic and totally soul-slanted menu would do to ride the river with.

One last thing is needed to complete the trip: a slice of sweet potato and banana pie. Despite the store-bought crust, this strange-sounding combo is a densely rich twist on an old standard, with mashed bananas blended into a fall-flavored sweet potato filling. Ultimately, it's whipped perfection. Jump on it like a duck on a june bug. Years from now, it will be the fondest memory of a strange but beautiful journey to the land of Leo.

"BECAUSE I WAS BORN IN THE SOUTH, I'M A SOUTHERNER. IF I HAD BEEN BORN IN THE NORTH, THE WEST, OR THE CENTRAL PLAINS, I WOULD BE A HUMAN BEING."

—CLYDE EDGERTON,
NORTH CAROLINA NOVELIST

# Ms. Ann's Southern-Style Cooking

##### 86 South Portland Avenue
##### Bet. Fulton Street & Lafayette Avenue
##### Fort Greene, Brooklyn
##### 718-858-6997
##### Cash Only

##### Main Courses: $7–$9

Past a quaint row of brownstones in this peaceful Brooklyn neighborhood stands a towering Southern monument: a larger-than-life figure known simply as Ms. Ann.

To pass through the faded storefront façade is to enter a bygone era. Handwritten signs "Please do not stand here" and "No credit! Please do not ask," signed "Ms. Ann," set the hospitable but steadfast house rules. A single blower cuts the heat of the hardworking kitchen while two ceiling fans are motionless against a pressed tin background. A scratchy AM radio blares. And only a well-worn Formica-topped counter separates customer and cook.

Ms. Ann smiles a greeting as cast-iron skillets and metal pots simmer away on the stovetop behind her. Lemony iced tea with ice tray cubes quenches the thirst while Ms. Ann points to the chalkboard menu and awaits a decision. Depending on the day, plump spareribs, thin and crispy pork chops, bones-and-all fried Atlantic croaker, or just about the best pan-fried chicken ever created by God or man or Southern belle can be yours for the asking. Heavily stewed and generously spiced black-eyed peas, collards, string beans, white rice with chicken gravy, or creamy, paprika-colored potato salad are the old-timey sides. To aid in sopping, each dinner comes with a hunk of deep dish cornbread, whose flour-infused, biscuitlike flavor defies description.

Generous wedges of hearty sweet potato pie with a hand-sculpted crust or an amazing chocolate-iced yellow cake emerge from a rattling icebox. Each of the day's meats can also be a sandwich to take home—on white bread, bone-in, and wrapped in a big square of stiff wax paper—if you're of a mind to think ahead.

A customer ambles up to the window, leaning in to discuss Ms. Ann's recent vacation and how much he missed her cooking. She carries on a neighborly chat, but her eyes never leave the fragrant batch of chicken she's carefully turning. Behind her, a woman checks her watch and waits to place a take-out order. All in Ms. Ann's own sweet time. Soon as she stirs that mess o' greens...

COLLARDS ARE OFTEN COOKED IN A SALT PORK-LACED, VINEGARY LIQUID CALLED "POT LIKKER." ONCE THE GREENS ARE SPOONED OUT, POT LIKKER IS SERVED AS SOUP WITH CORNBREAD FOR—WHAT ELSE?—SOPPIN'.

# NINTH STREET SOUL KITCHEN

████████████████████████████████████

337 E. 9TH STREET
BET. FIRST & SECOND AVENUES
212-473-0242
MAJOR CREDIT CARDS

MAIN COURSES: $10–$14

**F**inding Ninth Street Soul Kitchen can be tricky. That's because it's a "nights only" operation that shares a space with its better-known, "days only" alter ego, Ninth Street Market (also the only name on the sign out front). Still, the diminutive dining room is always crowded. This delectable little enterprise stays full with minimal hoopla because it has inspired a faithful following.

From the railroad tenement floor plan to the exposed pipes and radiator, the place is unpretentiously shabby chic. It's spruced up with hanging plants, starched tablecloths and benches lined with velvet pillows in shades of burgundy and ochre. Wegman-like photos of the owner's Boston terrier, Hercules, line the walls, along with a smattering of painted window frames and kitchen tools. Candlelight provides a golden glow.

Beyond a plate of rustic skillet cornbread, the simplicity ceases. The cuisine, inspired by the chef's Kentucky roots, is an artful blend of Old South ingredients and culinary creativity. For starters, lowly grits are mixed with red peppers, seared into buttery, finger-sized cakes, and piled with a mushroom ragout; sweet potato pancakes are topped with cinnamon-spiked applesauce; salmon croquettes get dressed up with dill remoulade.

Entrees are equally adventuresome, from the catfish dusted with cornmeal and pistachio to the ribeye glazed with Kentucky bourbon sauce and sprinkled with cracked black pepper. In the hands of Ninth Street, plain ol' pork chops and applesauce blossoms into two thick and tender cuts covered in tart fried apples, soft onions, and tomatoes and a pungent but subtle Georgia peanut sauce. Then two country cooking methods are fused in the fried chicken breast topped with Ninth Street's own barbecue sauce. And "our famous" chicken-fried steak is deserving of any and all accolades. Unlike the deep-fried chopped chuck

found on other menus, this is a delicately battered, medium-well steak sliced into strips and lightly doused in cream-based pan gravy.

Daily desserts like blueberry cobbler are homespun goodness, but it's Ninth Street's more inventive concoctions that make it distinctive. It's the rare soul kitchen that can twist and update the serendipitous flavors of the South into something altogether exciting and new.

# OLD DEVIL MOON

511 E. 12TH STREET
BET. AVENUES A & B
212-475-4357
MAJOR CREDIT CARDS

MAIN COURSES: $10–$16

The tune "Old Devil Moon" sprang from Finian's Rainbow, a musical set in a fictitious Southern state called "Missitucky." What name could be more appropriate for a divine dive dishing out grub with all the razzle-dazzle of a truck stop?

The place is a charming collection of clutter, as if every souvenir from every road trip ever taken has been nailed up or laid out. Tramp art and schoolroom maps cover the walls. Japanese lanterns, five-and-dime roses, and a disco ball dangle from the ceiling. A ceramic plaque inscribed to "Renee," lewd fairy tale etchings, and books with titles like *Hell is a City* load down the endless tchotchkes shelf. The tables and chairs are classic HoJo. A Niagara Falls honeymoon suite is more subdued than this fun-filled tack-o-rama.

Meals begin with a dish of crusty bread and a tiny, pungent Cheddar cheese ball. Try Hank W.'s crawfish pie instead or the Whistle Stop-worthy fried green tomatillos, thick cornmeal-crusted slices served with a Thousand Islandish sauce. Shrimp or crawdads come "sizzled" in "platonic-," "hellfire-," or "satanic-strength" ancho-chipotle sauce.

Main courses include Bayou-influenced jambalaya and swamp gumbo, but DFC ("Devil's fried") chicken or the "last wish" steak dinner (misdemeanor or death-row size) is the way to go. The melt-in-your-mouth, chicken-fried steak is an incredibly tender pan-fried cut of beef with rosemary-spiked cream gravy, crudely mashed potatoes and a crisp, mayo-free slaw. The true knockout, however, is genuine, cured country ham, and the deliriously salty slabs are shored up by a farm-fresh mixture of sauteed greens and cowpeas. The accompanying syrup-glazed skillet pone is novel, but the yams on the side leave something to be desired.

The finishing touch is a soup mug full of cobbler, with peaches as fresh as a Georgia orchard, dizzying autumnal seasonings, and flaky squares of crust. A fat slice of chocolate layer cake with white icing is also enticing, while the pecan pie is chock-full of chopped nuts and minimal Karo syrup.

Everything from grits to greens gets the royal treatment under that Old Devil Moon, and ol' time country cooking rules every howling night.

# ORLEANS

▪▪▪▪▪▪▪▪▪▪▪▪▪▪▪▪▪▪▪▪▪▪▪▪▪▪▪▪▪▪▪▪▪▪▪

**1438 THIRD AVENUE**
**BET. 81ST & 82ND STREETS**
**212-794-1509**
**MAJOR CREDIT CARDS**

**MAIN COURSES: $10–$18**

**O**rleans is the Upper East Side's only Louisiana creation, and it is far different from most of New York's Cajun/Creole eateries. It's not an ode to bayous so much as an artful take on the multicultural cooking methods of its mother city.

In keeping with the neighborhood's patented style, the decor has a tried-and-true Italian feel (it's a uniquely East Side quirk to surround foods from Ethiopian to esoteric with Mediterranean hues). A wavy wood bar backed with oceanic-blue tiles dominates the room, while floor-to-ceiling windows open it up. Votives and pendant lighting provide an orange glow across yellow-washed walls. Quaint, if not exactly Anne Rice.

Mediterranean swank gives way to a menu loaded with quirky backwoods titles for what turns out to be elaborate cuisine. Try appetizers like the peel 'n' eat "barnyard boiled" shrimp and "John Boy's" jambalaya, cubes of chicken and andouille in a hearty brown sauce over tomato-tinged rice. Orleans' specialty is the ambrosial yet fiery Louisiana blue-crab cakes on a mound of roasted corn relish and pale-green remoulade sauce, which deservedly took home first prize in a *Gourmet* magazine contest.

The Southernisms continue with the "Baptist church beer battered" fried chicken breast with jalapeño cheese, mashed potatoes, and "Maw Maw's" daily version of homestyle meatloaf. Succulent redfish comes coarsely crusted with seasoned pecans, anointed with a peppery sauce, and served with vibrant greens and an Acadian wild and white rice mixture. The customary crawfish étouffée and po' boys with fried oysters, catfish, or shrimp are on the menu, but the must-have entree is the Lafayette-bronzed and chile-rubbed-and-dusted pork chop, served with a moist square of wild mushroom bread pudding and fresh-cut creamed corn blended with red peppers and a vibrant hint of tequila. Whiskey pecan pie, filled with mounds of finely chopped nuts and resting on a star-shaped swirl of blueberry sauce, is a marvelously crumbly ending with a flavor reminiscent of good, homemade fruitcake (not the one that's been passed around for generations).

In a decidedly un-Southern domain, Orleans stands out both for bucking territorial convention and serving innovative and inspired Creole comestibles.

# PEARSON'S TEXAS BARBECUE

▰▰▰▰▰▰▰▰▰▰▰▰▰▰▰▰▰▰▰▰▰▰▰▰▰▰▰▰▰▰

**5-16 51ST AVENUE**
**BET. VERNON BLVD. & 5TH STREET**
**LONG ISLAND CITY, QUEENS**
**718-937-3030**
**CASH ONLY**

**MAIN COURSES: $5–$14**

City ordinances, fire codes, and space restrictions prevent most New York City barbecue restaurants from having real hardwood pits. Sure they can use electric or gas versions, throw in some wood chips or add liquid smoke to their hearts' content, but aficionados know nothing equals hours of hickory-smoked cooking. Whether your idea of barbecue is beef, pork, lamb, or links—never mind the infinite types of sauce—few disagree with the notion that crafting the real thing is a time-consuming, time-honored process. Pearson's Texas Barbecue has a pit. A real pit. 'Nuff said.

Five minutes from Grand Central finds you in front of the nondescript barbecue hut. In warm weather, the backyard holds picnic tables next to that heaven-scented pit. Inside, a built-in bench and wood tables sit under scores of rave reviews, publicity ops, and a billboard-size photo of three butt crack-bearing Bubbas on barstools, "all the way from Austin" to try Pearson's eats.

Who could blame them? From a kitchen consisting of a few burners, deep fryers, and stainless-steel roll-away counters, the constantly busy staff doles out meat, meat, and more meat. Pearson's throws everything into its pit—chicken, brisket, pork shoulder, sausage, and racks of ribs—and it all emerges seared until nearly black on the outside, ringed with smoky goodness at the edges, and utterly juice-filled at the center. All come as a sandwich or in bulk, and their wonderfully woodsy aromas softly twist any arm into trying a bit of everything. There are side dishes like the blissful onion rings, but the meat's the reason you're here.

The pork shoulder, sliced before your eyes, and the meaty short ribs (half-a-pound each) are the clear winners, especially when doused with the habanero-heated "mean" sauce. The chopped brisket is also neatly transformed from a bullheaded cut of beef to a tender temptation mixed with a sweet, tomato-based sauce. Pearson's version of North Carolina pulled pork is mixed with the same tomato-y sauce, and a sweet-and-sour approximation of vinegar sauce is thrown in on the side.

Pearson's is unimpeachable. That's why lines form in the early afternoon, with every race, religion, and creed yearning to eat real pit-cooked barbecue. That should be an inalienable right of all Americans—including New Yorkers.

# THE PINK TEA CUP

▀▄▀▄▀▄▀▄▀▄▀▄▀▄▀▄▀▄▀▄▀▄▀▄▀▄▀▄▀▄

### 42 GROVE STREET
### BET. BEDFORD & BLEECKER STREETS
### 212-807-6755
### CASH ONLY

### MAIN COURSES: $11–$15

At first blush, The Pink Tea Cup is a hybrid of a Good & Plenty box and a Mary Kay Cadillac, done up with contrasts of its signature color and jet black. The cotton-candy hue covers everything from the vinyl banquettes to the tile floors. Were it not for the mouth-watering scents blanketing the landscape, you'd swear this was the local Dippity-do Beauty Parlor.

This is a 40-year-old place where the staff actually opens the door and welcomes you when they spot you coming. Country breakfasts are served all day long. A jukebox and a ringing pay phone provide the atmosphere. And food orders go from your mouth to the waitress' ears to Dot's kitchen within a matter of seven seconds and some serious shouting. This is Southern hospitality, as they say, in the pink.

Dinners initially seem pricey, but—considering the bounty soon crowding the tiny tabletop—they're worth it. The all-inclusive meal starts with a bowl of refreshingly simple shredded lettuce and cabbage that falls somewhere between crunchy coleslaw and tossed salad. Homemade soup of the day follows, like tummy-warming chicken with chunks of carrot, celery, and egg noodles.

Then move on to the all-around amazing fried or smothered pork chops or chicken. Adventurous diners looking to go whole hog must have the honest-to-goodness ham hocks or braided chitterlings (for soul connoisseurs, not the faint of heart). Or dig into the crunchy pieces of cornmeal-fried catfish with grits or rice and gravy. Impeccable little bowls of squash, macaroni and cheese, or a corn, okra, and tomato mixture complete the meal. Dinner includes the amazing, cinnamon-spiked bread pudding or—no joke—Jell-O, which is refreshingly fun. Still, those bodacious, heavily-frosted cakes on the counter scream out, "Take me with you!" Hear and obey.

The Pink Tea Cup neither puts on nor puts up with airs. As with your mama's house, check any attitude at the door and slide on some rose-colored glasses.

CHITTERLINGS—"CHITLINS" TO MOST SOUTHERNERS—ARE LAUDED BY MANY, CRINGED AT BY OTHERS. THE TOWN OF SALLEY, S.C., HONORS THEM WITH AN ANNUAL "CHITLIN STRUT" FESTIVAL. CHITLIN MARKET AND CO. (800-933-2448) SELLS 90 TONS OF THEM A YEAR, MUCH OF THAT BY MAIL. WONDERING WHAT THEY ARE? TURN TO SOUTHERNSPEAK (PAGE 114).

# THE SAVANNAH CLUB

▮▮▮▮▮▮▮▮▮▮▮▮▮▮▮▮▮▮▮▮▮▮▮▮▮▮▮▮▮

2420 BROADWAY AT 89TH STREET

212-496-1066

MAJOR CREDIT CARDS

MAIN COURSES: $10–$15

I t's not often you can recognize a New York restaurant from blocks away because it sports a picket fence out front. It's also unusual to enter a Manhattan eatery and hear more Southern drawls per square foot than in the crowd outside the Today show. Then there's the "Ladies in Hats" rule of thumb: When ladies in hats, looking as if they've just left church, frequent a Dixieland-dedicated dining room, it's got to be good. Like way down yonder in Georgia, such is life at the Savannah Club.

Savannah Club's cuisine is old-fashioned country cooking with a New South spin. The fried okra appetizer is cornmeal-battered nirvana, spiced up with a horseradish, sour cream, and tomato dip. Equally amazing are the hot Southern fried oysters with a green-onion tartar sauce. And if the buttermilk biscuits with honey butter don't vanish as soon as they hit the table, ya' ain't human.

Huge portions of griddle-fried ham steaks and mama's fried chicken—battered just a little bit differently and served with creamy gravy, mashed potatoes, and leafy collards—rival the offerings of a church picnic. The same goes for the musky dirty rice and not-too-sugary candied yams. Finally, the house specialty, chicken and dumplings, is a stick-to-your-ribs classic, a deep bowl of hearty broth, whole pieces of sliding-off-the-bone chicken, and fat, sticky flour dumplings. It could make even a native New Yorker long for an icy day. Desserts run the gamut from sweet potato pie with honey custard sauce to peach cobbler to the ever-popular bananas Foster with double-chocolate ice cream.

Savannah Club conjures up images of Gothic mansions, moss-draped oaks, magnolia blossoms, and the lilting tunes of Johnny Mercer. When you sit facing the south wall, with its faded hues, African-American art, and cattail motif, it's easy to imagine you're steps away from Monterey Square. As for the disco-era bar, TV sets, and neon rings along the north wall—look away, look away. Oh, well, the city of Savannah is known for its eccentricities, too.

IF A TASTE OF SAVANNAH LEAVES YOU PANTING FOR MORE, PICK UP A COPY OF MIDNIGHT IN THE GARDEN OF GOOD AND EVIL, JOHN BERENDT'S PORTRAIT OF THE ECCENTRICITIES AND UNDERBELLY OF THIS GORGEOUSLY GOTHIC GEORGIA TOWN. FOLLOW THAT UP WITH HIDING MY CANDY, THE AUTOBIOGRAPHY OF MIDNIGHT'S BREAKOUT CHARACTER, THE LADY CHABLIS. THE DOLL EVEN HEATS UP THE KITCHEN WITH A CHAPTER OF HER FAVORITE RECIPES, INCLUDING "BITCHIN' BISCUITS," "TITILLATING TATERS," AND "SMACK Y'MAMA'S RIBS."

# SAZERAC HOUSE

**533 HUDSON STREET AT CHARLES STREET**
**212-989-0313**
**MAJOR CREDIT CARDS**

**MAIN COURSES: $11–$20**

With its Cajun cuisine and family table, home-style sensibilities, every day at Sazerac is a Louisiana Sunday. The 30-year-old restaurant—housed in an historical West Village farmhouse that dates back to 1826—is filled with the charm of real tin ceilings, creaky wood floors, and the constant scent of food in the air. It's a cozy cottage that feels like Grandmama's house.

Best of all, Sazerac proves quantity and quality can coexist, something normally found only at Aunt Wyladine's kitchen table. Like that favorite aunt, the friendly, seasoned servers chat, laugh, and never interrupt the endless flow of iced tea and corn bread sticks. Start the feast with steamed Creole mussels and slices

FINE FOODS & DRINKS

of fiery andouille sausage, huge barbecued shrimp with sweet corn fritters, or the more traditional Cajun popcorn shrimp with a sauce for dipping.

As a main meal, the gigantic bowl of jambalaya overflows with salty tasso ham, andouille, chunks of chicken, and shrimp. Pan-seared crab cakes, the house specialty, are truly amazing: flaky crusts on the outside, smooth, white crab meat in the middle. Though this dish is smolderingly spiced, it's made even hotter by two kinds of thick, orange remoulade sauce. The crab cake also comes as a sandwich with black beans, creamy slaw, and Cajun, spice-dusted chips on the side.

And those are the "simple" portions. A few dollars more buys a "complete" meal, which adds a salad or soup to the already-overcrowded tabletop. Then, if the body is willing, top it all off with a traditional Southern dessert such as rich, chocolate Mississippi mud cake, bread pudding drizzled with whiskey, or the not-so-Southern, but fabulously sinful, banana cheesecake, with an Oreo crust, caramelized bananas, and tons of chocolate.

Of course, no trip to Sazerac should end without a sip of its namesake, New Orleans' famous Sazerac cocktail. The ice-cold bourbon, bitters, and anisette mixture has been a French Quarter favorite for more than 140 years. With its feet planted firmly in Louisiana traditions, Sazerac House should be serving its home cooking for at least that long.

"THIS TOWN CONSUMES MORE ALCOHOL THAN ANY OTHER PLACE ON EARTH—BECAUSE WE START EARLIER. DRINKING A RAMOS FIZZ OR A SAZERAC WITH BREAKFAST IS CONSIDERED NORMAL BEHAVIOR."
—ELLA BRENNAN,
NEW ORLEANS RESTAURATEUR

# SHARK BAR

307 AMSTERDAM AVENUE
BET. 74TH & 75TH STREETS
212-874-8500
MAJOR CREDIT CARDS

MAIN COURSES: $12–$18

"Shark Bar" is a misnomer. It conjures up visions of sharkskin-suited hucksters, all toothpicking their pearly whites as the Jets gain territory on a big-screen television mounted to the wall. Thankfully, Shark Bar trancends that imagery.

The series of rooms housing this adventuresome kitchen is wonderfully comforting. Heavy, velvet drapes separate the small dining areas, lending privacy to snug booths and creating dramatic scarlet billows against mustard-yellow walls. Found throughout are dark wood floors, ceiling fans, and exposed-brick adorned with black-and-white photos of Harlem in the '30s, Miles Davis, and a family wedding portrait. Even the lighting is warm. It is tasteful and instantly relaxing.

Even more tasteful is the Southern revival menu, with its array of familiar favorites that are authentic yet innovative. Baskets of toasty biscuits and sweet potato muffins incite the first feeding frenzy, but save room for the main attraction: seafood. Start off with scallops and grits, salmon croquettes with Cajun mayonnaise, or the beguilingly juicy deep-fried strips of Georgia catfish with paprika-laced tartar sauce and a hot-as-Hades chile dip.

The ocean theme continues with the main courses, which include a fried seafood combo, shrimp étouffée, and seafood okra gumbo with shrimp, crab, fish, and scallops. The mighty meatloaf is a plainspoken meal. Here, the unheralded suburban standard is updated with ground turkey, a silky brown gravy, and scads of chopped green olives. The smothered pork chops are also stick-to-your-ribs, hearty fare, especially when accompanied by piping hot vegetables, which are slightly sweet and stewed with smoked turkey wings instead of fatback. Be sure to try chunky, pickle-packed potato salad and light macaroni and cheese. And the chicken-fried steak arrives with no batter and no gravy; not chicken-fried, just a normal steak.

Finish up with apple crunch pie, sweet potato cheesecake, or the walnut-fudge brownie, an eye-popping square served à la mode with a strawberry perched on top. The Uptown Combo, by the way, is a bargain that includes appetizer, entree, and dessert. For ferocious appetites only.

# SOUL FIXINS'

**371 W. 34TH STREET AT NINTH AVENUE**
**212-736-1345**
**CASH ONLY**

**MAIN COURSES: $5–$7**

**W**est of the Empire State Building and nearby Penn Station, attractions like Madison Square Garden, Macy's, and a mélange of neon storefronts play host to people from every corner of the world. Soul Fixins' ingeniously taps into that on-the-move market with ultraquick country cuisine as an alternative to burgers and pizza.

The Berry brothers' brainchild began as a delivery-only operation dishing out Southern standards from an apartment. The enterprise was such a successful alternative to the old standbys, the guys eventually set up a no-frills storefront amidst the 34th Street mayhem. Soul Fixins' was alive and kickin'.

Though they still do mainly takeout and delivery, the dining room is fine for a quick meal. It's easy-to-clean simplicity: industrial gray indoor/outdoor carpeting and fire engine red tiles. Seating is elbow to elbow, like pigs in a poke.

Everything at Soul Fixins' is billed as "lunch," and the pickin's range from gravy-smothered chicken to homemade meatloaf to a vegetarian plate made up of four sides. And what sides! Chunky, burnished orange slices of yams, vinegary chopped collard greens, and baked macaroni and cheese drowning in wholesome, mild Cheddar are the stand-out accompaniments.

Finger-licking entrees are deep-fried, darkly browned quarters of chicken, wings drizzled with honey, barbecued ribs, and, best of all, cornmeal-dipped whiting fillets. This crackling, deep-fried soul classic is whipped up on the spot, then the two platter-size portions are ready for dousing with tartar sauce or an ultrawicked Tabasco concoction. Squares of dense corn pone the size of a child's building block finish off the "meat and two" specials, but don't leave without grabbing a hunk of mighty fine sweet potato pie from the constantly replenished stack of clear plastic containers by the register.

Instead of waiting in line at some fast-food chain with slack-jawed "yoots" droning, "Next," consider the alternative: hearty helpings served by the sharp staff at Soul Fixins'. Or would you like fries with that?

"RC AND A MOON PIE, PLEASE." IN THE '50S, THE COMBINATION OF A BOTTLE OF FIZZY ROYAL CROWN COLA AND A MOON PIE SANDWICH OF CRUNCHY COOKIES, MARSHMALLOW FILLING AND CHOCOLATE ICING BECAME THE SOUTH'S MOST POPULAR "FAST FOOD" LUNCH.

# SOUL FOOD KITCHEN

▪▪▪▪▪▪▪▪▪▪▪▪▪▪▪▪▪▪▪▪▪▪▪▪▪▪▪▪▪

84 KINGSTON AVENUE AT DEAN STREET
BEDFORD-STUYVESANT, BROOKLYN
718-363-8844
MAJOR CREDIT CARDS

MAIN COURSES: $7–$15

**B**anana Pudding. Those are the first words emblazoned across the Soul Food Kitchen awning. A counterman with a high-tech headset—à la Madonna—stands on the sidewalk, directing diners toward their destination: one side of the building for takeout, the other for sit-down. A few steps over is yet another sign, this one in gold foil: Now Serving Frog Legs. This must be the place.

Inside, a friendly-but-harried waitress rushes glasses of lemony, sweet tea to groups of churchgoing families. Some surround the salad bar, a folksy conglomeration of iceberg lettuce, tomato slices, broccoli, and dressings. Wide, comfortable booths are set underneath Chinese restaurant-style mirrored panels, glass-and-brass fixtures, and shiny, Oriental wallpaper.

Once settled in a booth with napkins from a tabletop dispenser in hand, the fun begins. Munch on a massive block of almost-unsweetened cornbread. Chopped pork barbecue, dreamy fried chicken, boiled chitterlings and oxtail await, but how about those frog's legs? The stack of cornmeal-overlaid hind quarters arrives looking like the muscular lower halves of toy action figures. Yes, they do taste like chicken, but the snowy flesh is chewier, saltier, and more succulent than its feathered friend. The whiting is equally delicious, with a crackling coating on slender fillets.

With these country wonders come some amazing sides. The big-elbow-macaroni and cheese swims with tangy Cheddar and almost zero custard, and the collards are finely chopped and smoky. Black-eyed peas are slowly steeped to plump perfection.

A dessert order of a butter pecan milk shake, an individual, real-crusted sweet potato pie, and the advertised banana pudding gets "a look," followed by a warning: "You're not gonna be eating all that pudding today." No kidding. The butterscotch-hued finale is a seven-inch take-out container packed with eggy, from-scratch pudding, tons of banana, and easily half a box of vanilla wafers. Oh, and it's out of this world. Several heaping spoonfuls later, half remains. That aluminum container is no accident—bag it up, and you're on your way with tonight's midnight snack and dreams of more banana pudding.

# SYLVIA'S

■▲■▲■▲■▲■▲■▲■▲■▲■▲■▲■▲■▲■▲■

### 328 LENOX AVENUE
### BET. 126TH & 127TH STREETS
### 212-996-0660
### MAJOR CREDIT CARDS

### MAIN COURSES: $8–$16

She's everywhere! Sylvia Woods has worked her way from waitress to owner of a national enterprise. Her restaurant is a Harlem landmark that has inspired a cookbook, a line of food products, and an expanding chain of Sylvia's across the country ("Would you like grits with that?"). Tour buses steadily unload chattering foreigners on 125th Street to head, en masse, for Sylvia's; the Queen of Soul Food has universal appeal. Inside, her smiling face is on everything from her supermarket products to a poster-sized photo in which she greets her customers with open arms. Welcome to Planet Sylvia.

In its more than 35 years, Sylvia's has grown in size as well as popularity, swallowing up every space surrounding the original. Consequently, the decor consists of a '50s-style lunch counter, a '60s wood-and-brick rumpus room, a '70s fern bar, and an early-'80s tropical paradise room. It's as if The Bradys, The Ropers, and The Cleavers are all under one roof.

A Sunday gospel brunch is the best time to experience Sylvia's. While singers orbit with cordless mikes, the congregation digs into eggs with salmon croquettes, thick-slab bacon, Southern-style hash, country ham, or syrup-slathered hotcakes. Of course, the breakfasts come with homemade biscuits and buttery, molten grits.

Non-breakfast items like fried chicken quarters or pork chops—thinly floured and fried until reddish-brown and glistening—are accompanied by shiny-topped, cakey cornbread. Her smothered chicken and chops are also faultlessly fried before being covered in hearty gravy and served with sides such as tangy pickled beets, gherkin-infused, almost-creamy potato salad, and plump candied yams that taste just like pumpkin pie. The "world famous, talked about" ribs arrive blanketed in Sylvia's own bottled barbecue sauce.

For a heavenly dessert, go for the fluorescent yellow banana pudding topped with crisp vanilla wafers. When the check arrives soon after, be aware that a 15% gratuity is automatically tacked on (though the super staff deserves that much and more).

Sylvia's popularity makes it wildly busy, yet Ms. Woods always does an unparalleled job of serving down-to-Earth eats to billions and billions. And another tour bus arrives...

SYLVIA'S IS GROWING FAST, BUT NOTHING GROWS LIKE KUDZU. THIS ORIENTAL VINE WAS INTRODUCED TO THE SOUTH IN THE '30S TO HALT EROSION, AND IT PROMPTLY BLANKETED THE REGION (AT A RATE OF UP TO A FOOT A DAY). DIXIE WRITER JOHN SHELTON REED OFFERS KUDZU AS A DEFINITION OF THE SOUTH'S BOUNDARIES, SINCE IT PROSPERS BELOW THE OHIO AND POTOMAC RIVERS BUT NOT IN SOUTH FLORIDA OR WEST TEXAS.

# T.J.'S SOUTHERN GOURMET

**92 CHAMBERS STREET**
**BET. BROADWAY & CHURCH STREET**
**212-406-3442**
**MAJOR CREDIT CARDS**

**MAIN COURSES: $6–$10**

In the heart of New York's hustle-and-bustle downtown business district, one would not normally expect to find sumptuous, slow-cooked Southern food. Lunch here is often a deli sandwich or a pizza slice inhaled while walking. T.J.'s Southern Gourmet breaks the mold with down-home fare cooked all morning in preparation for the mad dash of the noon hour.

Since 1990, T.J.'s has been regaling the suit-and-tie crowd with meals that put the typical lunchtime "same old, same old" to shame—and rightly so. Yet it's as lightning-quick as its competitors, with a front area built for takeout: mile-long steam counter, stacks of  paper bags, and waxy cups to facilitate choosing and running (their new Jamica, Queens location takes it a step further, with the word "Express" tacked on to the restaurant's name).

Time permitting, however, the dining room is not to be missed. The room is a salmon-tinted, urban-throwback treat. It's not unusual to see disheveled prosecutors pulling up captain's chairs for a lunch meeting or groups of secretaries congregating under the "Tiffany" fixtures, all against a backdrop of gold Mylar streamers and framed ads with TV icons like Tony the Tiger.

Almost instantly, hot cornbead arrives on styrofoam saucers with syrupy-sweet iced tea close behind. All the food is cooked in back then toted through the dining room to be put on public display, but it arrives surprisingly hot. The boneless, cornmeal-dipped whiting is superb, snow-white flesh in a crunchy, salty crust. Superfirm meatloaf (with the added twang of sausage) makes a dandy sandwich, as do the old-fashioned ham hocks on white bread. Smothering, however, is what T.J.'s does best: deep-fried cuts of pork and poultry quarters concealed under a mellow black pepper gravy.

Long grain rice with the same silken sauce is a peerless Southern side. Sweet slaw and almost-mashed potato salad brim with mayo. T.J.'s mac and cheese is almost custardless, making it crumblier than most but just as good. For dessert, you could grab a piece of smooth sweet potato pie or homemade cake, but go for the supersweet banana pudding. With massive banana slices, a slew of crumbly vanilla wafers and minimal pudding content, this is some of the best the city has to offer.

T.J.'s happeningest time is lunch. That's when their freshest offerings can be found, food that's been fussed over for hours. Bet the hot dog cart on the corner can't make that claim.

# TRAMPS CAFE

▼▲▼▲▼▲▼▲▼▲▼▲▼▲▼▲▼▲▼▲▼▲▼▲▼▲▼▲▼▲▼▲

**45 W. 21ST STREET**
**BET. FIFTH & SIXTH AVENUES**
**212-633-9570**
**MAJOR CREDIT CARDS**

**MAIN COURSES- $14–$22**

**B**ar food? Not here. Despite being adjacent to the well-known live music venue of the same name, Tramps Cafe is not a popcorn shrimp munchfest for the clubgoers next door. On the contrary, Chef Abe de la Houssaye of Lafayette, Louisiana, creates a serious dining experience with genuine Acadian cooking.

Tramps is housed in a hollow, high-ceilinged space typical of the neighborhood. The decor is unassuming: exposed air-conditioning ducts spanning the room, a colossal wood bar, moss-gray tin ceilings, ebony-glossed floors, and walls the texture and shade of particleboard. Then there are the flags. Flags from practically every civic group and state in the nation cover the walls and unfurl from the ceiling. That's it.

While zydeco music wails and the upstairs neighbors pound away like the World Wrestling Federation (there's a fencing school upstairs), dig into the flown-in-fresh shellfish boil or pickled shrimp. The crab gumbo—in a finely spiced brown stock with rice on the side to add as desired—is a radiating bowl of warmth that could take the chill off an iceberg. Beans get their own heading on the menu: red beans and rice with turkey tasso, black bean chili, and Hoppin' John with andouille sausage.

Plump oysters fried in light peanut oil are piled high on an unmanageably large French roll to form a savory, overstuffed "Peacemaker's" po' boy, served with excellent Cajun-spiced fries. The Cajun shellfish boil of crawfish, shrimp, and crab is a seasonal luxury, while Deep South favorites such as fried or barbecued chicken breasts are available every day. Flaky farm-raised catfish comes three exquisite ways—blackened with butt-

kicking tartar sauce, fried, or in a broth of stewed tomatoes, onions, and bell pepper over white rice, known in Lafayette as "courtbouillon." All the entrees arrive with a bowl of collard slaw (shredded greens are added to the mix). And the selection of homebaked sweets depends on the dessertmaker's mood. Will she make that popular rum pecan pie today?

Tramps Cafe strikes a balance between elegant eats and a bit of the Wild Cajun for an Acadian feast and a hopping good time.

ACCORDING TO LORE, THE ACADIANS' BELOVED CRAWFISH FOLLOWED THEM FROM NOVA SCOTIA TO LOUISIANA IN THE 1700S. TO REWARD THE MUDBUGS' LOYALTY, THE CAJUNS TOOK TO EATING THEM WITH BUTTER AND A NICE ROUX.

# TWO BOOTS

▰▰▰▰▰▰▰▰▰▰▰▰▰▰▰▰▰▰▰▰▰▰▰▰

**37 AVENUE A AT 3RD STREET**
**212-505-2276**
**MAJOR CREDIT CARDS**

**MAIN COURSES: $8–$11**

Two Boots is mostly known as a thriving local pizza chain, offering TV-themed pies ("The Mel Cooley," "The Newman") that easily outshine the garden variety "slice." But the anchor restaurant is a shotgun marriage of Cajun and Italian, an unlikely combination that has its roots in the Italian influence on Creole cooking during the last century. Now the boot-shaped regions of Italy and Louisiana pair up.

Two Boots' interior is a playful mishmash of styles geared toward their ever-present kid population. The curvaceous counter is a hermetically sealed treasure trove of gewgaws a child would keep in a shoe box, crayon art serves as menu covers, and pint-size cowboy boots occupy a window sill. Red vinyl banquettes—suitable for climbing and conniptions—line the room. Background music ranges from Gershwin to P-Funk.

While the kiddos dig into pizza and a boot-shaped mug of root beer, adults can feast on ragin' Cajun. For a sampling of appetizers, start with the "pu-pu platter," combining crawfish-black bean cakes, Creole popcorn, and jambalaya pies. The cakes are mashed beans and meaty crawfish, rolled in cornmeal and fried until golden. The empanadalike jambalaya pies, about the size of oyster shells, are flaky pastry pockets filled with seafood and rice. And the Creole popcorn is a pile of tiny shrimp (not crawfish, as with the Cajun version), deep-fried, and served with a tomato-tarragon sauce.

Dinners include seafood filé gumbo with shrimp, crabmeat, oysters, and catfish all stewed and spiced, red beans and rice with jalapeño cornbread, and po' boys with fried catfish or a combination of Italian sausage and savory Cajun andouille. Chicken "zuzu" is perhaps the best choice, a butter-bronzed breast of chicken filled with a stinging Creole oyster stuffing that bites you hard several moments after a forkful. Blackened catfish supreme is charred rather than seared in Cajun spices, but a covering of sassafras-laden shrimp étouffée adds more than enough heat. If the pizza mood strikes, have the Bayou feast pie with barbecue shrimp, crawfish, andouille, and jalapeño peppers. The finale is chocolate pecan pie, peanut-butter pie, or daily specials like cream cheese-iced red velvet cake.

This is also one of the few New York restaurants to serve New Orleans' famous chicory coffee, with its bittersweet endive twang. A cup of that Louisiana treat is the perfect way for the adults in the crowd to cool their heels while the kids get their Two Boots kicks.

# VIRGIL'S REAL BBQ

**152 W. 44TH STREET**
**BET. BROADWAY & SIXTH AVENUE**
**212-921-9494**
**MAJOR CREDIT CARDS**

**MAIN COURSES: $11–$20**

When the concept-courting owners of Ollie's and Carmine's decided to traverse the Southland in search of the best of the BBQ Belt, they did Manhattan a huge favor. What sprang from their wanderings is Virgil's, a barbecue shrine so satisfying it defies the logic of those who believe corporate-owned eateries simply cannot be good. Here's the exception.

Just off Times Square, Virgil's is inundated with tourists, pre-theaterites, and transplanted Bubbas looking for a fix (the blazing-orange neon sign cries out "BBQ" from afar). Fortunately, the two-level dining room can accommodate the crowds. And what a lively space it is, blending '50s coffee shop service, a Western steakhouse feel and the muted tones of a family-style cafeteria. Not surprisingly, the walls are covered with mementos of the big road trip, and place mats are maps of the South with legendary barbecue huts pinpointed like state capitals. On each paper mat is a terry cloth towel for a napkin: a preview of what's to come.

Virgil's buttermilk biscuits with gravy are a must to begin every meal, though the huge onion rings with blue-cheese dressing will also do you just fine. Boneless fried chicken or a single, oversized, smoky Texas sausage link makes for a classic po' boy. The cured ham dinner is a superb blend of salty pork and an unusually sweet sauce. And country staples such as fried shrimp, catfish, and potato chip-breadcrumb-cracker-laden Georgia chicken-fried steak pop up among the entrees.

But Virgil's appeal is in the barbecue, which is oven-smoked with fruitwood and oak. Generously proportioned spareribs are spiced to the verge of being black. Pulled pork is piled high and varied in color from charred to pink, as the good stuff always is. That Virgil's serves Owensboro lamb—the sliced, roast beeflike barbecue native to Kentucky—is further proof they've done their homework. The gotta-have-it side dish? Smoky and syrupy Memphis baked beans, without a doubt. All the meats come by the pound or as sandwiches topped with crisp, mustardy slaw. Regional sauce choices are mustard, vinegar, and Memphis mild or hot. If this isn't enough of a pig-out, the dessert sampler platter of pecan, peanut butter, Key lime, and chocolate chess pies along with banana pudding should drive any sane person 'round the bend.

Virgil's is a cornucopia of barbecue in its every cross-cultural form, and they do it all brilliantly and abundantly. Hell, they even put their smoked goodies on a salad. For the health-conscious.

# WILSON'S BAKERY & RESTAURANT

▪▪▪▪▪▪▪▪▪▪▪▪▪▪▪▪▪▪▪▪▪▪▪▪▪▪▪▪▪▪▪▪

**1980 AMSTERDAM AVENUE AT 158TH STREET**
**212-923-9821**
**CASH ONLY**

**MAIN COURSES: $8–$27**

Diners are nonexistent in the Southland. There are plenty of places where waitresses in polyester pantsuits navigate with a coffee pot in one hand and a pitcher of tea in the other; where locals shoot the breeze over daily doses of burgers and grits; where the smell of bacon grease lingers in the air all day. The highways and tiny towns of Dixie are home to the most colorful examples of the species. But they are "coffee shops," "pancake houses," or "truck stops," never "diners." Even with a name like Raynell's Home Cooking Diner, no one would ever call it that. The North is Diner Land. Wilson's is as close as Manhattan gets to a Southern diner, though never shall the twain truly meet.

Wilson's meets the criteria for New York diner decor, with its glassed-in addition, vinyl seating, and autographed photos of every "celebrity" who has ever passed through the doors. At the end of a sit-and-serve counter with swiveling barstools is a tremendous display case filled to one-tenth its capacity with chocolate and coconut layer cakes shaped like loaves of bread, sweet potato pies, and a few cookies.

With its immense laminated menu, Wilson's elemental Southernness doesn't jump off the page; it is filled with items as wholly American as apple pie. But then you spot the homemade biscuits and corn muffins being halved, buttered, and toasted on a hot griddle behind the counter. Next, it's the breakfast column, with its bowls of hominy grits and dark-brown, ultracrisp, and raved-about salmon patties with an accompaniment of waffles.

The dinners present lots of possibilities, starting with beef liver and bacon, baked Virginia ham with applesauce and smothered steak (on Tuesdays and Sundays). Center-cut pork chops come fried until golden and mouth-wateringly juicy. Deep-fried, flour-and-pepper-encrusted, utterly tender chicken breasts fill the air with Sunday-dinner perfume. Unlike the steamed broccoli or canned corn veggie choices most diners offer, Wilson's piles on limas, slow-stewed collards, rice and gravy, or mashed sweet potatoes.

Mach speed Manhattan eating and inherently slow Southern cooking coexist as closely as can ever be expected at Wilson's. The restaurant doesn't doll itself up like Tara or dress down to resemble a trailer park. It simply mixes the best of New York with the best of the South.

"THE WAY FOLKS WERE MEANT TO EAT IS THE WAY MY FAMILY ATE WHEN I WAS GROWING UP IN GEORGIA. WE ATE TILL WE GOT TIRED."
—ROY BLOUNT, JR.
SOUTHERN HUMORIST

# SOUTHERNSPEAK

**Andouille:** spicy, smoked pork sausage made in Louisiana and based on the French original of the same name.

**Brunswick stew:** a meat-based stew that is usually so thick it can be eaten with a fork. Depending on the region, the stew may include chicken, pork, or even squirrel, but it nearly always contains potatoes, onions, tomatoes, and seasonal vegetables such as corn. It is also highly-spiced and often served as an accompaniment to barbecue. Both Brunswick, Georgia and Brunswick, Virginia claim to be its birthplace.

**Chicken-fried:** any meat dipped in milk (or buttermilk), rolled in a mixture of flour, salt, and pepper, and fried until crunchy. Chicken-fried items usually come smothered in thick cream gravy.

**Chicory:** endive root that is roasted, ground, and added to coffee; a Louisiana specialty.

**Chitterlings:** a.k.a. **chitlins**; braided, inside-out pig intestines that may be served boiled or fried, hot or cold. This is a dish that's not to be sniffed at, darlin'.

**Cowpeas:** another name for black-eyed peas.

**Crawfish:** a.k.a. **crayfish**, **crawdads**, **crawdaddies**, **mudbugs**; fresh water crustaceans that look and taste like a cross between lobster and shrimp. Widely used in Louisiana cooking.

**Étouffée:** translation: "smothered"; usually refers to the Acadian crawfish version, with mudbug tails and fat, parsley, onions, and tomatoes. The best étouffées are rich and smooth with crawfish fat, not flour.

**Filé:** the Creole name for powdered sassafrass; used as a thickener for stews and soups.

**Geechie:** a slang term for the African American Gullahs who inhabit many of the sea islands off the coast of North Carolina, South Carolina, and Georgia. Their unique culture is a mix of African, Spanish, French, and Southern heritages.

**Grits:** a.k.a. **hominy**; stone ground corn that, when boiled in salty water for 20 minutes, has the consistency of oatmeal; usually served for breakfast, topped with anything from butter and cheese to bacon and gravy.

**Gumbo:** a stew with a variety of meats that is usually thickened with okra (the name comes from the African word for okra, "quingombo").

**Haint green:** a hue of bluish green believed to ward off evil spirits; commonly used on the front porches of homes in the coastal Deep South, presumably to make ghosts pass on by.

**Hog maws:** hog "jowls"; anything from the mouth to the gullet of a pig.

**Hoppin' John:** a stewed mixture of black-eyed peas, chunks of pork, and white rice served on New Year's Day for good luck (and any other time just for good eatin').

**Jambalaya:** rice, oysters, tasso ham, andouille, and giblets cooked together as a sort of Creole paella; usually rather dry, not heavily sauced.

**Kudzu:** the vine that ate the South; see the bottom of page 103 for more frightening details.

**Lowcountry:** refers to South Carolina's coastal region and, more specifically, its seafood-rich cuisine.

**Macque choux:** a mixture of corn, tomatoes, onions, and green peppers; often served with Creole food.

**Mint julep:** seen by many as the South's cocktail of choice, particularly when sitting on a plantation home's front porch or watching the Kentucky Derby. A potent mixture of bourbon or sour mash, spearmint-laced syrup, shaved ice, and a substantial sprig of mint usually served in a silver julep cup.

**Okra:** a.k.a. **the pod of the gods**; a semi-slimy oblong vegetable that Southerners slice and fry, stew, or add to soupy dishes as a thickening agent. A beloved Dixie staple.

**Oxtail:** the tail of an ox or cow; it is skinned, sliced, stewed, and usually served smothered in gravy.

**Po' boy:** a.k.a. **poor boy**; originally, a New Orleans hero sandwich that was mainly roast beef and French bread; nowadays, it can contain anything from oysters to chicken with spicy condiments or gravy and the usual sandwich fixin's.

**Pone:** an ol' timey term for cornbread (usually skillet bread).

**Ramos Fizz:** a famous New Orleans libation made with gin, powdered sugar, cream, vanilla, orange flower water, lemon juice, lime juice, seltzer water, and an egg white. The key is shaking the concoction until frothy.

**Receipts:** recipes, in the Old South vernacular.

**Red-eye gravy:** a salty sauce made from country ham drippings and water; a popular topping for grits and biscuits.

**Remoulade:** a Cajun sauce usually made with mayonnaise, mustard, cayenne, tarragon, sweet pickles, capers, parsley, chevril, and, most importantly, horseradish.

**Smithfield ham:** a salty, smokehouse-cured pork delicacy made exclusively in Smithfield, Virginia.

**Wonder Bread:** to most Southerners, this brand is the God-given bread of choice for sandwiches.

# Virtual Vittles

HERE'S A SAMPLING OF THE SOUTHERN COMESTIBLES,
COMMUNITIES, AND CULTURE WE'VE FOUND ONLINE.

**The Amazing Story of Kudzu**
(http://www.sa.ua.edu/cptr/kudzu.htm). Everything
you'd ever want to know about the scourge of the
South.

**BourbonStreet**
(http://www.geocities.com/BourbonStreet). A community of websites devoted to Southern food, music, and
culture.

**Byrd Cookie Company**
(http://www.byrdcookiecompany.com).
Savannah's famous treats delivered to your door.

**Cajun Brew**
(http://rampages.onramp.net:80/~ndronet).
All Cajun, all the time, from recipes to lore.

**Chitlin Market and Company**
(http://www.chitlinmarket.com). Chitterlings by mail.

**Goo-Goo Clusters** (http://googoo.com).
An ode to the famous Southern snack.

**Grits** (http://www.grits.com).
What they are and why we love 'em.

**Krispy Kreme** (http://www.krispykreme.com). For
those who just can't get enough of those glistening puffs.

**The Lexington Collection**
(http://www.ipass.net/~lineback/lex.htm).
Barbecue from A to Z.

**Moon Pie** (http://moonpie.com).
The fascinating history of this sweet little sandwich.

**Piggly Wiggly** (http://www.pigglywiggly.com).
The low-down on the Pig.

**Southern American Cuisine**
(http://southernfood.miningco.com).
Down-home recipes, chat, links, and the on-line
newsletter, "Beyond Biscuits."

**Southern Living Online** (http://southern-living.com).
The "best of the South" from the eternally-popular
magazine.

**Tabasco** (http://www.tabasco.com).
History, contests, and ordering info from the
McIlhennys of Avery Island, Louisiana.

**Texas Monthly Online**
(http://www.texasmonthly.com).
"The National Magazine of Texas" and its Internet
"ranch."

**Y'all.com** (http://www.yall.com).
"The Webzine of the South," covering every conceiv-
able Southern topic "like kudzu."

**Y'all NYC**
(http://www.geocities.com/BourbonStreet/Delta/5963).
Our own corner of the South—Mayberry-on-the-
Hudson.

# GRIT LIT

▪▪▪▪▪▪▪▪▪▪▪▪▪▪▪▪▪▪▪▪▪▪▪▪▪▪▪▪▪▪▪▪▪▪▪

FOR THOSE IN PURSUIT OF FURTHER SOUTHERN TRUTHS, WHAT FOLLOWS IS A LIST OF RECOMMENDED READING. WHILE COMPILING OUR GUIDE, THESE ARE THE BOOKS WE REFERRED TO, LEARNED FROM, LAUGHED AT, AND FLAT-OUT LOVED.

**B. SMITH'S ENTERTAINING AND COOKING FOR FRIENDS** by B. Smith (Artisan, 1995). The African-American Martha Stewart adds a Southern twist to dinner party planning and more.

**CHARLESTON RECEIPTS** by The Junior League of Charleston, Inc. (1994). The oldest cookbook of its kind in print; an indispensable kitchen companion for fans of Lowcountry cuisine.

**CULTURE SHOCK! USA—THE SOUTH** by Jane Kohen Winter (Times Edition Pte. Ltd., 1996). The tourists' guide to venturing below the Mason-Dixon line.

**DORI SANDERS' COUNTRY COOKING: RECIPES AND STORIES FROM THE FAMILY FARM STAND** by Dori Sanders (Algonquin Books of Chapel Hill, 1995). The author of *Clover* and *Her Own Place* reminisces about country living, the family peach farm, and her beloved Aunt Vestula's recipe collection.

**EATING, DRINKING, AND VISITING IN THE SOUTH** by Joe Gray Taylor (Louisiana State University Press, 1982). A scholarly, historical, and yet entertaining look at the roots of Southern hospitality.

**ENCYCLOPEDIA OF SOUTHERN CULTURE** edited by Charles Reagan Wilson and William Ferris (University of North Carolina Press, 1989) The heavily-researched—and mighty heavy—1,634 page, definitive reference work on all things Southern.

**GRACE THE TABLE: STORIES AND RECIPES FROM MY SOUTHERN REVIVAL** by Alexander Smalls, with Hettie Jones and a foreword by Wynton Marsalis (HarperCollins, 1997). The owner of Cafe Beulah delves into his rich family history and whips up out-of-this-world Southern Revival specialties.

**HAVING IT Y'ALL: THE OFFICIAL HANDBOOK FOR CITIZENS OF THE SOUTH AND THOSE WHO WISH THEY WERE** by Ann Barrett Batson (Rutledge Hill Press, 1988). An amusing, detailed manual on what it takes—and takes out of you—to be a good Southerner.

**MRS. HILL'S SOUTHERN PRACTICAL COOKERY AND RECEIPT BOOK** by Annabella P. Hill (University of South Carolina, 1995; originally self-published, 1872). The original Julia Child; a Georgia housewife whose detailed cooking instructions were all the rage in nineteenthth century America.

**NEVER EAT MORE THAN YOU CAN LIFT (AND OTHER FOOD QUOTES AND QUIPS)** by Sharon Tyler Herbst (Broadway Books, 1997). A compendium of commentary from people who must like to talk when their mouths are full.

**ON THE NIGHT THE HOGS ATE WILLIE (AND OTHER QUOTATIONS ON ALL THINGS SOUTHERN)** edited by Barbara Binswanger and Jim Charlton (Dutton, 1994). Hundreds of droll things to say while sipping a mint julep.

**ROY BLOUNT'S BOOK OF SOUTHERN HUMOR** edited by Roy Blount, Jr. (W. W. Norton & Company, 1994). A hefty, hysterical 150-entry anthology that runs the gamut from "A Position on Whisky" by Noah Sweat to Zora Neale Hurston's "Mules and Men," all with sparkling introductions by the always-wily Blount.

**SERIOUS PIG: AN AMERICAN COOK IN SEARCH OF HIS ROOTS** by John Thorne, with Matt Lewis Thorne (North Point Press, 1996). An "army brat raised on Yankee food" explores the culinary wonders of the South.

**SIDE ORDERS: SMALL HELPINGS OF SOUTHERN COOKERY AND CULTURE** by John Egerton (Peachtree Publishers, 1990). Egerton collected so much information for Southern Food—and continued to collect more—he ended up dishing out seconds to his hungry admirers with this recipe-filled continuation.

**SOUL FOOD: CLASSIC CUISINE FROM THE AMERICAN SOUTH** by Sheila Ferguson (Grove Press, 1989). Recipes and family lore by a Philly native who learned her considerable culinary skills from Southern relatives.

**SOUL FOOD: RECIPES AND REFLECTIONS FROM AFRICAN-AMERICAN CHURCHES** by Joyce White (HarperCollins, 1998). When this food editor found herself living in New York City and longing for the comfort cuisine of her Alabama home, she began visiting Harlem churches for the next best thing. These are the stories and recipes that sprang from her soul searching.

**SOUTHERN FOOD: AT HOME, ON THE ROAD, IN HISTORY** by John Egerton (University of North Carolina Press, 1993). History, restaurants, recipes, lively conversation. This is the pinnacle of Southern food writing, an encyclopedic, mouth-watering volume that reads like a letter from home.

**SPOONBREAD AND STRAWBERRY WINE: RECIPES AND REMINISCENCES OF A FAMILY** by Carole and Norma Jean Darden (Main Street Books, 1998). Two sisters travel the South in search of their roots and come home to New York with photos, lore, and recipes ranging from sweet potato pudding to face cream.

**SYLVIA'S SOUL FOOD: RECIPE'S FROM HARLEM'S WORLD-FAMOUS RESTAURANT** by Sylvia Woods and Christopher Styler (Hearst Books, 1992). The Queen of Soul Food on the cuisine that made her restaurant legendary.

**THE TASTE OF COUNTRY COOKING** by Edna Lewis (Random House, 1976). A now-classic cookbook from the foremost authority on authentic Southern food.

**WHISTLING DIXIE: DISPATCHES FROM THE SOUTH** by John Shelton Reed (Harcourt Brace Jovanovich, 1990). Side-splitting essays like "How to Get Along in the South: A Guide for Yankees" and "The Garden of Eatin'." A Southern must-read.

**WHITE TRASH COOKING** by Ernest Matthew Mickler (Ten Speed Press, 1986). Includes such trailer park masterpieces as Mona Lisa Sapp's Macaroni Salad, Miz Bill's Bucket Dumpling, and Oozie's Okra Omelet. Need we say more?

# INDEX BY
# NEIGHBORHOOD

# ACKNOWLEDGEMENTS

Thanks to Helene Silver and Melisa Coburn at City & Company; our parents, Patricia Cook, Gene and Jerry Wyatt; our grandmothers, Patsy Andrews and Nova McGaughey; our brothers and sisters, Angie, Christy, Dustin, Kristopher, Joel, and David; our supportive and fact-finding friends, Stan Allen, Tony Barnes, Robert Hernandez, Stuart Johnson, Steven "Grit Lit" Lewis, Kevin McClendon, and Melissa Stanton; everyone else who lent everything from their time to their excitement to this project—Mary Ann Crenshaw, Lisa Dellwo, Alec Gerster, Anne Hearn, Kay McDuffie, Stephanie Rath, The Belles on Eight—and, especially, Richard William Rhodes, for his steadfast support.

# NEW YORK COOL & CLASSIC

Would you like to receive City & Company's 25 Cool and Classic Places to Go in New York? It's free. Just share with us your favorite New York spot and return the form to us via mail, fax, or e-mail.

So the next time someone says, "What do you want to do this weekend?" maybe you'll surprise them!

**NAME** _____

**ADDRESS** _____

_____

**FAVORITE NEW YORK SPOT** _____

_____

_____

_____

_____

**RETURN TO :**

City & Company
22 West 23rd Street
New York, New York 10010
Fax 212.242.0415
E-mail cityco@bway.net

# ABOUT THE AUTHORS

━━━━━━━━━━━━━━━━━━━━━━━━━

**BRUCE LANE** is an agented screenwriter and accomplished cook. He is a South Carolina native who was weaned on Orange Crush and Goo Goo Clusters by a family of strong women...a truly Gothic Southerner. Lane lives out-of-water in Manhattan and has just completed his third feature-length script.

**SCOTT WYATT** was born and raised amidst the piney woods and back bayous along the Arkansas-Louisiana-Texas state lines, at the "buckle" of the Barbecue Belt (and he claims to have the waistline to prove it). He moved to New York to work on Madison Avenue—his heart lead him back to Main Street.